THE CLAUDIA SANDERS DINNER HOUSE

of Shelbyville, Kentucky

COOKBOOK

by

Cherry Settle

Tommy Settle

Edward G. Klemm, Jr.

Library of Congress Catalog Number is 78-74905

ISBN 0-89144-074-7

Fifth Printing

To
Colonel Harland Sanders and his Wife,
Claudia.

They have been our Mentors and
Our Inspiration

TABLE OF CONTENTS

ABOUT THE AUTHORS

Tommy Settle (Thomas Quentin Settle, Sr.)

Born in Owensboro, Ky. 1942

Attended University of Alabama

Former State Amateur Golf Champion
(Still holds title as youngest man ever to win Men's Amateur Golf Championship).

Won the State Junior Golf Championship same year.

Ran the Officers Club while stationed in Germany when in the Army.

Cherry Settle

Born in Louisville, Ky. 1943
Mother of Tommy, Jr. 3 yrs. old and Jennifer 4 mos. old
Started modeling at age 16. Taught modeling and charm.

Started acting career in Kentucky in a movie named "The Great Race".

Did bit parts, stand-in, double and extra work in Hollywood, California for 3 years. Some of the movies worked in include "Never Too Late", "Clambake" (with Elvis Presley), "Harlow", "Marriage On The Rocks" (with Dean Martin, Frank Sinatra), "Hotel", "Chamber of Horrors" and T.V. Shows "Run For Your Life", "F.B.I.", "Mission Impossible", "I Spy" and "F. Troop".

Returned to Kentucky and started working for "Kentucky Fried Chicken" as National Sales Hostess. Job was to train the sales hostess (the young lady that serves you your chicken) throughout the entire United States including Alaska and Hawaii. Met the Colonel who later offered to sell "Claudia Sanders Dinner House" to the Settles.

About the Authors

Edward G. Klemm, Jr.

Born in Louisville, Ky. 1910. Son of Roberta K. Klemm, a published poet and songwriter, and Edward G. Klemm, Sr., a Louisville attorney.

Graduated from University of Chicago in 1932. Taught in Louisville Junior and Senior High Schools and was a newspaper reporter before opening own real estate and insurance business in Louisville.

With his Mother, Roberta K. Klemm, has written music which has been published both in the United States and in Vienna, Austria.

Is a member of ASCAP, a Life Member of the National Association of American Composers and Conductors, a Life Member of the J. B. Speed Art Museum.

Has traveled extensively and sold photographs to magazines.

Two previously published books: "Precious Heritage", a novel and "I Wonder Why", a book of poems.

INTRODUCTION

On the first of June, 1968, Claudia Sanders opened the Claudia Sanders Dinner House near Shelbyville, Kentucky. The restaurant is in the building originally used by her husband, Colonel Harland Sanders, as office and warehouse for his Kentucky Fried Chicken operation, and is located on the grounds of the Colonel's former home.

After running the restaurant for five years, Claudia Sanders decided to franchise the operation and awarded the first franchise to Tommy and Cherry Settle.

Because of the excellent quality of its meals the restaurant has gained, not only a national, but an international reputation.

It is in response to the many requests from customers that this book is offered and we hope that it may help bring into your kitchen the magic flavors associated with the Claudia Sanders Dinner House.

WEIGHTS, MEASURES AND EQUIVALENTS

Should you become involved with measurements in the metric system, the following tables and information will be of help:

WEIGHTS

Ounces	Grams
1/3	10
1/2	14
7/8	25
1	28.3 (30)
1-3/4	50
2	56.6
2-1/2	71
3	84.9 (85)
3-1/2	100
4-1/2	125
16 (1 pound)	453

LIQUID MEASURES

Fluid ounces	Centiliters
1/6 (1 teaspoon)	1/2
1/3	1
1/2 (1 Tablespoon)	1-1/2
5/8	1-2/3
1 (1 fluid ounce)	2.96
8 (1 cup)	23-1/2
16 (1 pint)	47
32 (1 quart)	95
33-1/2	100 (1 liter)

TEMPERATURES

Fahrenheit (°F.)	Centigrade (°C.)
200	93
212	100
225	107
250	121
275	135
300	149
325	163
350	177
375	190
400	205
425	218
450	232
475	246
500	260
525	274
550	288

CONVERSION FORMULAS

To convert Fahrenheit degrees into Centigrade degrees, subtract 32 from the Fahrenheit degrees; multiply by 5, and divide by 9.

To convert Centigrade degrees into Fahrenheit degrees, multiply the degrees Centigrade by 9, and divide by 5; add 32.

EQUIVALENTS

3 teaspoons	is equivalent to	1 tablespoon
2 tablespoons	is equivalent to	1 liquid ounce
4 tablespoons	is equivalent to	1/4 cup
16 tablespoons	is equivalent to	1 cup
2 cups	is equivalent to	1 pint
2 pints	is equivalent to	1 quart
4 quarts	is equivalent to	1 gallon
16 ounces	is equivalent to	1 pound

Metric		**U. S.**
1 milliliter	equals	.034 ounce
1 liter	equals	33.81 ounces
.61 milliliters	equals	1/8 teaspoon
1.23 milliliters	equals	1/4 teaspoon
2.47 milliliters	equals	1/2 teaspoon
3.7 milliliters	equals	3/4 teaspoon
4.94 milliliters	equals	1 teaspoon
14.78 milliliters	equals	1 tablespoon
3.69 milliliters	equals	1/8 ounce
7.39 milliliters	equals	1/4 ounce
14.78 milliliters	equals	1/2 ounce
22.17 milliliters	equals	3/4 ounce
29.57 milliliters	equals	1 ounce
29.57 milliliters	equals	1/8 cup
59.14 milliliters	equals	1/4 cup
118.28 milliliters	equals	1/2 cup
177.42 milliliters	equals	3/4 cup
236.56 milliliters	equals	1 cup
473 milliliters	equals	1 pint
946 milliliters	equals	1 quart
1.89 liters	equals	1/2 gallon
2.83 liters	equals	3/4 gallon
3.78 liters	equals	1 gallon

Dry measurement in grams   U. S.

.54 grams	equals	1/8 teaspoon
1.09 grams	equals	1/4 teaspoon
2.19 grams	equals	1/2 teaspoon
3.28 grams	equals	3/4 teaspoon
4.38 grams	equals	1 teaspoon
1.77 grams	equals	1/8 tablespoon
3.54 grams	equals	1/4 tablespoon
7.09 grams	equals	1/2 tablespoon
10.63 grams	equals	3/4 tablespoon
14.18 grams	equals	1 tablespoon
3.59 grams	equals	1/8 ounce
7.39 grams	equals	1/4 ounce
14.18 grams	equals	1/2 ounce
21.34 grams	equals	3/4 ounce
28.35 grams	equals	1 ounce
453.56 grams	equals	1 pound
28.34 grams	equals	1/8 cup
56.69 grams	equals	1/4 cup
113.39 grams	equals	1/2 cup
170.08 grams	equals	3/4 cup
226.78 grams	equals	1 cup

SOUPS
AND APPETIZERS

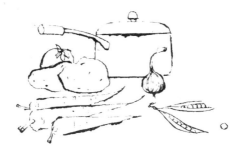

The best party meatballs you will ever serve. Our guests just rave about these.

COUNTRY HAM AND SAUSAGE BALLS

1 pound ground Claudia Sanders Kentucky Country Ham
1/2 pound pork sausage
1/2 cup cheese-and-garlic-flavored croutons (finely ground in blender)
1 egg, beaten
5 drops onion juice
1/3 cup milk

1. Preheat oven to 400° F.
2. Mix all ingredients together, blending thoroughly.
3. Roll into bite-size balls.
4. Place balls in baking pan large enough to hold them without touching each other.
5. Pour meatball sauce over meatballs.
6. Bake at 400° F. for one hour, or until meatballs are firm.

Makes 55 meatballs.

MEATBALL SAUCE

2 tablespoons brown mustard
1 cup brown sugar
1 cup white vinegar
1/2 cup apple juice

1. Combine all ingredients and place in a saucepan.
2. Cook over high heat to a boil. Stir well.
3. Remove from fire and pour over meatballs while hot.

A perfect appetizer.

CHEESED MUSHROOMS

3 pints fresh mushrooms
10 strips crisp bacon (crumbled)
3/4 cup mayonnaise
1 medium-sized onion (minced)
1/2 cup grated sharp cheese
1 cup mozzarella cheese
salt or seasoned salt to taste

1. Preheat oven to 325° F.
2. Remove stems from mushrooms.
3. Wash mushroom caps in salted water.
4. Place in shallow, buttered cooking pan, cup side up.
5. Mix mayonnaise, onion and bacon; salt to taste (we recommend using a seasoned salt).
6. Fill mushroom caps with mayonnaise mixture.
7. Mix grated cheeses and sprinkle over mushrooms.
8. Bake at 325° F. for 15 minutes.

Serves 10 to 12.

An appetizer that can be prepared the day before.

CHICKEN LIVER PÂTÉ

8 strips Claudia Sanders Country Bacon
2 pounds chicken livers
5 tablespoons rendered chicken fat
1 medium-sized onion (chopped)
1/2 teaspoon salt
1/4 teaspoon black pepper

1. Brown bacon in large skillet over medium heat to obtain fresh bacon grease.
2. Remove bacon strips from skillet (save them for some other use)
3. Add rendered chicken fat to bacon grease in skillet.
4. Add onion and fry until tender.
5. Add chicken livers.
6. Continue cooking for 10 minutes or until livers are done. Turn livers occasionally while cooking.
7. Add salt and pepper and stir well.
8. Remove from heat and let cool.
9. When cool, blend in blender to make pâté.
10. Refrigerate and serve cold with toast points or crackers and side dish of finely chopped, uncooked onions.

Serves 12.

A good snack item—especially for you weight watchers.

PICKLED EGGS

12 to 16 eggs
2 cups cider vinegar
2 tablespoons granulated sugar
1 teaspoon salt
1 teaspoon mixed pickling spices
1 medium sized onion (sliced)
1 garlic clove

1. Hard cook eggs. Set aside while preparing pickling mixture.
2. Mix vinegar, sugar, salt and pickling spices.
3. Put in sliced onion and garlic clove.
4. Bring mixture to a boil; then simmer for 8 minutes.
5. Remove eggs from shell and pack in quart jars while hot.
6. Pour hot vinegar mixture over eggs.
7. Cover. Refrigerate and let stand for 2 days before serving

Serves 6 to 8.

We find these best served when icy cold.

A different meatball.

SURPRISE MEATBALLS

2 pounds ground beef
1 egg
1 tablespoon chopped onion
1 2-ounce jar pimiento-stuffed olives (whole)
1/4 cup pimiento-stuffed olives (sliced)
1/4 cup flour
2 tablespoons butter
1/4 cup milk
1 cup sour cream
1/2 cup grated sharp cheese
1-1/2 teaspoons salt
1/2 teaspoon black pepper
2 drops Tabasco sauce

1. Preheat oven to 400° F.
2. In a mixing bowl, mix ground beef, egg, onion, pepper and 1 teaspoon of the salt. Shape into balls.
3. Press a whole olive into each ball.
4. Coat balls with flour.
5. Melt the butter in a large skillet and brown the meatballs over medium heat until all outside of balls are browned. (If necessary, add more butter)
6. Remove meatballs to a 3-quart casserole. Set aside.
7. In the skillet in which you cooked the meatballs, put the milk and stir over low heat to scrape the drippings for about 1 minute.
8. Remove skillet from heat and add sour cream to the milk mixture.
9. Add the cheese, Tabasco drops, the 1/2 teaspoon salt and the sliced olives.
10. Pour this over the meatballs in the casserole.
11. Bake at 400° F. for 12 minutes, or until meatballs are done.

Serves 6.

Top off this Bean Soup with apple pie. That's what we do at the Claudia Sanders Dinner House of Shelbyville and call it our Bean Soup Special.

BEAN SOUP

4 cups Country Ham Stock (see Country Ham Stock recipe, page 196)
2 cups canned Great Northern Beans
1/8 cup chopped red pepper
1 teaspoon salt
1/8 teaspoon black pepper
1 cup chopped meat from ham hock (from preparing stock)

1. Mash one cup of the beans.
2. Add this and the cup of whole beans to the stock.
3. Put in the ham hocks, red pepper, salt, and black pepper.
4. Cook for about 15 minutes over medium heat.

Serves 4 to 6.

This delicious bean soup will really stick to your ribs.

BLACK BEAN SOUP

2 cups black beans
1 ham bone
1 small onion (finely chopped)
3 tablespoons cooked rice
1 bay leaf
1 small green pepper (chopped)
1 garlic clove (finely cut)
1 beef bouillon cube
2 ounces Sherry wine
salt and pepper to taste

1. Wash beans and soak for 12 hours, or overnight.
2. Put in cooking pot and cover with cold water.
3. Add bay leaf, garlic and ham bone and boil until beans are completely soft.
4. Add beef bouillon cube and green pepper.
5. Boil for another half hour.
6. Remove from stove and add Sherry wine, salt and pepper.

Serve with a garnish of rice on one side and finely chopped onions on the other.

Serves 8.

Fast, easy and good!

BLENDER CREAM OF CUCUMBER SOUP

3 cucumbers (peeled and coarsely chopped)
1 can chicken broth
1 cup half-and-half
2 spring onions (chopped)
1 stalk celery (chopped)
2 tablespoons melted butter
2 tablespoons flour
1 teaspoon salt
1/2 teaspoon black pepper
1/2 teaspoon monosodium glutamate

1. Place all ingredients in a blender and mix until smooth.
2. Refrigerate for at least 4 hours.
3. Serve with a little dill weed sprinkled on top and, if you prefer to add color, also sprinkle with grated lemon rind and finely chopped cucumber.

Serves 4.

Our version of a traditional Kentucky dish that is especially popular around Kentucky Derby time.

BURGOO

1 pound lean pork
1 pound lean beef
1 medium-sized hen (cut up for boiling)
1 gallon salted water
2 large potatoes
2 large carrots
2 medium-sized onions
1 cup peas (fresh or canned)
1 cup green beans (fresh or canned; cut in small pieces)
2 cups canned tomatoes
1/4 cup diced okra
1 cup chopped cabbage
1 medium-sized green pepper (diced with seeds removed)
1/8 teaspoon diced red pepper pod
1/3 cup tomato paste
1-1/3 cups V-8 vegetable cocktail
2 tablespoons chopped parsley
1-1/2 teaspoon salt
1/4 teaspoon black pepper
4 teaspoons Worcestershire sauce

1. Boil pork, beef and hen in salted water until done.
2. Drain, cool and remove chicken bones and skin.
3. Run meats through food grinder.
4. Put the meat and the one gallon water in a large cooking pot. Set aside.
5. Peel and dice the potatoes, onions and carrots.
6. Combine these with the okra, cabbage, peas, beans, tomatoes, green and red peppers and the parsley.
7. Add to the meat and water.
8. Put in the tomato paste and V-8 vegetable cocktail.
9. Season with the salt, black pepper and Worcestershire sauce.
10. Cook at a slow boil over moderate heat for 2-1/2 to 3 hours. Stir often.

Yields one gallon burgoo. Serves one Kentucky Colonel.

This soup is also delicious when prepared with small noodles instead of rice.

CHICKEN RICE SOUP

4 cups chicken stock (see Chicken Stock recipe, page 197)
1 cup diced white meat of chicken (from preparing the stock)
1 cup cooked rice
1 medium-sized onion, chopped fine
2 small carrots, chopped fine
1 cup finely chopped celery
1 teaspoon salt
1/8 teaspoon white pepper

1. Place onion, carrots, and celery in a cooking pot and cover with water.
2. Simmer for 1/2 hour.
3. Drain and set aside.
4. Season chicken stock with salt and pepper.
5. Add onion, carrots, celery, rice and diced chicken to stock.
6. Simmer over low heat for 20 minutes.

Serves 4 to 6.

A delicious and attractive one-dish meal.

COMPLETE MEAL SOUP

2 chickens (cut into pieces)
3 quarts water
1-1/2 tablespoons salt
10 whole peppercorns
1/4 of a red pepper pod (cut into small pieces)
1 onion (medium sized and diced)
5 very small carrots (cut into strips)
1 pint fresh whole green beans with ends trimmed (washed and drained)
2 medium sized zucchini squash (each cut into eighths)
1 stalk celery (sliced very thin diagonally)

1. Place chicken pieces, water, salt, peppercorns, red pepper pieces, and diced onion in a large kettle.
2. Bring to a boil and then turn down fire to simmer.
3. Cover loosely and simmer for one hour or until chicken pieces are tender.
4. Strain and cool broth.
5. Skim fat off broth.
6. Remove chicken pieces from broth.
7. Discard skin from chicken pieces.
8. Put chicken pieces back into broth.
9. Bring broth to boil again.
10. Place carrots to one side in kettle and celery to another and cook for 10 minutes.
11. Add green beans to another side and cook for 10 more minutes.
12. Add zucchini pieces to another side and cook for 10 minutes.
13. Serve in large bowl, placing chicken pieces in center surrounded by individual groups of the vegetables.
14. When serving, slowly add one cup of broth to each individual soup bowl.

Serves 6.

A tasty soup for your luncheon guests.

CREAM OF MUSHROOM SOUP

1/2 pound mushroom caps (chopped)
4 cups water
1/2 small onion (diced)
4 tablespoons butter
1/4 cup sifted flour
1/2 cup cream
1/4 teaspoon salt
1/8 teaspoon black pepper

1. Simmer mushrooms and onion in the four cups water for 20 minutes. Drain, reserving liquid.
2. Put through sieve or food mill, returning to liquid. Set aside.
3. Combine butter and flour.
4. Add to cream.
5. Add cream mixture to mushrooms.
6. Add salt and pepper.
7. Simmer for about ten minutes.

Serves 6.

If you like your soups rich, substitute cream for the milk in this recipe.

CREAM OF TOMATO SOUP

2 cups tomato juice
2 teaspoons finely chopped onions
2 tablespoons butter
1-1/2 teaspoons flour
1-1/2 cups milk
2 tablespoons granulated sugar
1 teaspoon salt
3/4 teaspoon white pepper

1. Melt the butter in a skillet. Add the flour and chopped onions. Cook until onions start to brown. Set aside.
2. Combine milk and tomato juice and cook over medium heat for 3 to 5 minutes, but do not bring to a boil.
3. Stir butter-flour mixture into the milk and tomato mixture.
4. Season with the salt and pepper.
5. Bring mixture to a simmer.
6. Add sugar and remove from fire.

Serves 4 to 6.

When your garden is plentiful, this is a pleasing summer soup.

GAZPACHO

1 large cucumber (peeled and diced)
4 ripe tomatoes (peeled and finely chopped)
1 small onion (finely chopped)
1 medium-sized green pepper (seeded and finely chopped)
1/4 cup olive oil
1/4 cup wine vinegar
2 cups tomato juice
1 teaspoon salt
1/2 teaspoon black pepper
1/4 teaspoon monosodium glutamate
pinch garlic salt

1. Mix all ingredients together in a mixing bowl.
2. Refrigerate for at least six hours.
3. Serve in iced serving bowls.

Serves 8.

There is no better introduction to a good meal than a bowl of onion soup.

ONION SOUP

8 cups water
2 cups chopped onions
1/4 cup cornstarch
1/4 cup beef stock base
croutons and Parmesan cheese to garnish

1. Cook onions in five cups of the water until they are transparent.
2. Add the beef base. Set aside.
3. Mix cornstarch into the balance of the water and boil for one minute.
4. Combine with the onion mixture and heat thoroughly.
5. Garnish with croutons and Parmesan cheese before serving. Serve hot.

Serves 8.

A cup of French Onion Soup will whet your appetite for the meal that follows. A bowl of it is a meal in itself.

FRENCH ONION SOUP

8 cups water
2 cups chopped onions
1/4 cup cornstarch
1/4 cup beef stock base
8 small toast rounds
8 slices mozzarella cheese, cut large enough to cover the entire top of the soup in the serving bowl.

1. Cook onions in five cups of the water until they are transparent.
2. Add the beef base. Set aside.
3. Mix cornstarch in the balance of the water and boil for one minute.
4. Combine with the onion mixture and heat thoroughly.
5. Place in individual oven-proof, bowl type, baking dishes (8) and float a round of the toast in each dish.
6. Cover the entire top of soup with slice of mozzarella cheese.
7. Place in broiler and broil until cheese melts slightly and starts to brown.

Serves 8.

This is a soup that will really hit the spot.

PEA SOUP

1 small potato (boiled until soft)
1 cup peas (fresh-cooked or canned)
1 teaspoon granulated sugar
1/4 teaspoon salt
1/8 teaspoon black pepper
1 cup milk
1 cup water
1 tablespoon flour
1 tablespoon butter
1 small onion (diced)

1. Cut potato into small pieces and run through grinder, or food mill, with the peas. Set aside.
2. Mix milk, water, sugar, salt and pepper together.
3. To milk mixture add the peas and potato mixture, together with the onion.
4. Thicken with the flour and butter and cook over moderate heat for one hour.

Serves 4.

Starr Wiecek gives an Old World flavor to her dinners with this soup.

POLISH SAUSAGE SOUP

1 double-link smoked Polish sausage
2 quarts water
3 heaping tablespoons flour
1 cup sour cream
3 garlic cloves (cut into small pieces)
3 teaspoons horseradish
1 teaspoon salt

1. Mix the flour, sour cream and salt and make into a smooth paste. Set aside.
2. Put the garlic and horseradish in the water. Cook the sausage in this water for 45 minutes.
3. Remove the sausage and set aside.
4. Bring the liquid to boiling again and then pour into the sour cream mixture and beat until smooth.
5. Serve in separate soup dishes.
6. The sausage can be cut into slices and placed in the soup according to one's individual taste. This is also very good when served with hard cooked eggs and dill pickles.

Serves 6.

This is a delicious cold weather soup.

POTATO SOUP

4 medium-sized potatoes
3 stalks celery (cut into small pieces)
1 small onion (grated)
3 cups milk
1 tablespoon flour
1/4 cup water
2 tablespoons melted butter
1 teaspoon salt
1/8 teaspoon black pepper

1. Cook potatoes and celery in boiling salted water for 30 minutes or until soft.
2. Drain and run through food grinder or food mill.
3. Add the milk and grated onion.
4. Mix the flour and water and add to the milk mixture.
5. Combine the melted butter, salt and pepper and add to milk mixture.
6. Bring soup to a boil and simmer for 15 minutes.

Serves 6.

SALADS

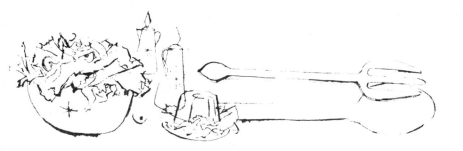

This tasty salad should always be prepared the day before you plan to use it.

BEAN SALAD

2 cups canned green beans
2 cups canned, cut wax beans
2 cups canned, dark red kidney beans
1/2 cup chopped green pepper
1/2 cup chopped onion
1/2 cup chopped pimiento
1/2 cup granulated sugar
2/3 cup vinegar
1/3 cup salad oil
1 teaspoon salt
1/4 teaspoon black pepper
1/4 teaspoon celery seed.

1. Drain and combine beans.
2. Add green pepper, pimiento and onion. Set aside.
3. Combine sugar, vinegar, salad oil, salt, pepper and celery seed and pour over beans. Mix thoroughly.
4. Refrigerate overnight.

Serves 6 to 8.

This salad is colorful as well as tasty.

CHERRY GELATIN SALAD

2 packages cherry-flavored gelatin (6-ounce size)
2 packages red raspberry-flavored gelatin (6-ounce size)
3 quarts boiling water
1/4 cup apple juice
2 cups frozen tart cherries (pitted & thawed)
2 16-oz. cans applesauce
1 cup sour cream
2-1/2 cups miniature marshmallows

1. Dissolve the four packages of gelatin in the boiling water.
2. Add frozen cherries, apple juice and applesauce.
3. Pour into large mold and chill until jellied.
4. Mix sour cream and marshmallows with an electric mixer at high speed until marshmallows are completely dissolved. (About fifteen minutes)
5. To release gelatin from mold, dip bowl in hot water for just a second.
6. Cover with marshmallow mixture.

Serves 14.

Note: When gelatin starts to set, stir to fold cherries and applesauce evenly throughout the mixture.

If you wish, you may use some dark meat of chicken in this salad.

CHICKEN SALAD

2 cups boiled white meat of chicken (cut into small cubes)
2/3 cup mayonnaise (see page 55)
1/3 cup whipping cream (whipped)
1/2 cup finely chopped celery
1/3 cup capers
fresh lettuce leaves

1. Add whipping cream to mayonnaise and beat to mix thoroughly.
2. Add chicken and celery to mayonnaise and mix completely.
3. Line a salad bowl with lettuce leaves and cover with chicken salad.
4. Garnish with capers and serve cold.

Serves 4 to 6.

This is a delightful combination salad for a cold lunch on one of those hot summer days.

CHICKEN SALAD WITH FRUIT

1 orange (seeded and sections cut in half)
1/2 cup seedless grapes, cut in half
1 medium-sized red-delicious apple (peeled, cored and seeded)
1/3 cup pecan, or almond, pieces
1 banana, sliced
2 cups chicken salad (see recipe above)
fresh lettuce leaves

1. Combine all ingredients thoroughly.
2. Line a salad bowl with the lettuce leaves and cover with the salad.
3. Serve cold.

Serves 5 or 6.

Try this for a change in salads.

COLD CARROTS

1 pound fresh cooked tiny whole carrots
1 10-ounce can tomato soup
1 cup granulated sugar
1/2 cup corn oil
3/4 cup vinegar
1 teaspoon prepared mustard
1 teaspoon Worcestershire sauce
1 medium-sized onion (chopped)
1 medium-sized green pepper (chopped)
a few drops Tabasco sauce
salt and pepper to taste

1. Combine all ingredients, except carrots, to make a marinade.
2. Drain carrots and place in a bowl or other container.
3. Pour marinade over carrots.
4. Cover and marinate overnight.

Serves 6 to 8.

The secret of this cole slaw is to chop the cabbage very fine.

COLE SLAW I

1 pound cabbage
1/3 cup granulated sugar
1-1/4 tablespoons tarragon vinegar
1-1/4 tablespoons vegetable oil
1 tablespoon finely chopped onion
1/3 cup mayonnaise
1/4 teaspoon salt
1/4 teaspoon black pepper
1/4 teaspoon celery salt

1. Core cabbage and chop very fine. Set aside.
2. Combine, in a blender, the sugar, vinegar, vegetable oil, onion, mayonnaise, salt, pepper and celery salt.
3. Mix this with the cabbage, combining thoroughly.
4. Chill and serve cold.

Serves 6 to 8.

We think cole slaw makes a nice hot weather salad.

COLE SLAW II

1 medium-sized head of cabbage (cored)
1 cup granulated sugar
1/4 cup cider vinegar
1/4 cup oil (vegetable or olive)
1 medium-sized onion, chopped very fine
1 cup salad dressing
1 teaspoon salt

1. Chop cabbage very fine. Set aside.
2. Combine vinegar, oil and salad dressing and mix thoroughly.
3. Add sugar and onions.
4. Season with the salt.
5. Combine with the cabbage and stir to mix completely.

Serves 4.

If you like, you can stuff tomatoes with this crab meat salad.

CRAB MEAT SALAD

1 cup canned crab meat
mayonnaise (we like to use our own. See page 55)
3/4 cup finely chopped celery
fresh lettuce leaves
paprika or chopped parsley to garnish

1. Combine crab meat and celery with enough mayonnaise to moisten and hold mixture together.
2. Place in mounds on lettuce leaves.
3. Garnish with paprika or parsley and serve.

Serves 2 or 3.

What a sandwich spread this makes!

EGG SALAD WITH BACON
AND COUNTRY HAM

6 hard-cooked eggs (grated, or finely chopped)
1/4 cup bacon bits (cooked crisp and crumbled)
1/4 cup ground Claudia Sanders Kentucky Country Ham
1 teaspoon onion (minced)
1/2 cup celery (finely chopped)
1/2 teaspoon seasoned salt
1/4 teaspoon Tabasco sauce
1/4 cup mayonnaise
1 tablespoon lemon juice or cider vinegar
paprika to garnish
6 stuffed olives (chopped or whole to top each serving)
Mix all ingredients thoroughly and sprinkle paprika on top. Garnish with the olives.
Makes approximately 6 servings or 6 sandwiches.

Add sunshine to your breakfast table.

FRESH FRUIT SALAD

2 grapefruits
2 pears
2 bananas
1 cup strawberries (cut in half)
1 cup shredded coconut
1 cup fresh pineapple (diced)

1. Peel grapefruit and cut in slices crosswise.
2. Remove seeds.
3. Core, but do not peel, the pears and cut into small pieces. Mix with coconut and pineapple.
4. Peel and slice bananas. Combine with strawberries.
5. Toss all ingredients together and serve chilled.

Serves 4.

Gladys Biggers tells us her fruit salad can be put in jars and frozen to be used later.

GLADYS' FROZEN FRUIT SALAD

12 teaspoons unflavored gelatin
6 cups canned fruit, drained (Save the juice.) Gladys uses peaches cut in small pieces and fruit cocktail.
1/2 cup cold fruit juice from the cans
2 cups hot fruit juice from the cans
6 tablespoons granulated sugar
1 teaspoon salt
1 cup mayonnaise
2 cups whipping cream (whipped)

1. Drain the fruit, saving the juice. Set aside.
2. Soften the gelatin in the cold fruit juice.
3. Heat the 2 cups fruit juice and add to cold juice.
4. Put in the sugar and salt, stirring until dissolved.
5. Chill until the mixture begins to thicken.
6. Beat the mayonnaise into the whipped cream and fold into the gelatin mixture.
7. Add the fruit, and place the mixture in a large salad bowl.
8. Refrigerate, stirring twice during the first hour. Then let set.

Makes 2-1/2 quarts.

Never did a Thanksgiving or Christmas go by that we didn't have this for dinner. We think it is the best we have ever tasted anywhere.

MOM'S CRANBERRY SALAD

1 package fresh cranberries (16-oz package)
1 whole orange
1 package red raspberry gelatin (3-oz size)
1 package orange-flavored gelatin (3-oz size)
1 cup chopped pecans
1-1/2 cups granulated sugar

1. Grind cranberries and whole orange (peel and all) in food grinder. Set aside.
2. Mix gelatins according to the directions on their packages.
3. In large mixing bowl, combine cranberry mixture, sugar, nuts and gelatins.
4. Pour into molds, or leave in bowl.
5. Refrigerate overnight, or until set.

Serves 8.

Potato salad always makes a good hot weather luncheon.

MRS. ORTHMAN'S POTATO SALAD

4 cups white potatoes (peeled, cooked and diced)
2 eggs (hard-cooked and diced)
1 cup chopped celery
1 cup chopped onion
1/2 cup stuffed olives (sliced and their juice)
1/4 cup French dressing
1/4 cup mayonnaise
1 teaspoon salt
1/2 teaspoon black pepper

1. Combine the French dressing and mayonnaise and use this to moisten the potatoes.
2. Season with the salt and pepper.
3. Add the eggs, celery, onions and olives.
4. Put in some of the olive juice for flavor to your taste.

Serves 4 to 6.

Colorful, easy to fix, and tastes delicious.

RED RASPBERRY SALAD

1 package orange gelatin (3-oz size)
1 package raspberry gelatin (3-oz size)
2 cups frozen red raspberries
1 #2 can applesauce
1 cup sour cream
2-1/2 cups miniature marshmallows

1. Dissolve both packages of gelatin in 1-1/2 cups boiling water.
2. Add berries and applesauce.
3. Stir and chill until molded.
4. In a separate dish mix sour cream and marshmallows; beat with rotary mixer for 15 minutes or until marshmallows dissolve.
5. Spread sour cream-marshmallow mixture on top of the salad.

Serves 10 to 12.

A hot weather dish that's good for a luncheon or as a snack.

SALMON SALAD

1 cup canned red salmon (7-3/4-oz. can)
1 hard-cooked egg (chopped)
1/2 cup celery (chopped fine)
1 tablespoon vinegar
1/4 teaspoon salt
1/8 teaspoon black pepper

1. Remove any bones from salmon.
2. Mash the salmon with a fork until it is smooth.
3. Add the vinegar, salt and pepper and combine well.
4. Add the egg and celery and blend thoroughly.
5. Serve on a lettuce leaf and with crackers.

Serves 2.

You can garnish this salad with strips of canned pimientos or sprinkle with paprika.

WALDORF SALAD

1 cup uncooked apple, cut into small pieces
1 cup celery, cut into small pieces
1 cup seedless grapes, cut in half
1/2 cup chopped pecans (or walnuts)
1/2 cup mayonnaise

1. Combine apple, celery, grapes and nuts.
2. Add the mayonnaise and stir to completely moisten the ingredients.
3. Serve on fresh lettuce leaves.

Serves 4 to 6.

Add zest to your meal. Try this different way of fixing spinach salad. The water chestnuts give it a certain crispness.

WILTED SPINACH SALAD

1 pound spinach (washed, dried and crisped)
2 hard-cooked eggs (coarsely chopped)
1/2 cup water chestnuts (thinly sliced)
2 tablespoons lemon juice
4 tablespoons olive oil
1 large, or 2 small, garlic cloves (chopped)
2 tablespoons soy sauce
1/2 teaspoon freshly cracked peppercorns
salt to taste

1. Cook olive oil and garlic over medium heat for 2 minutes.
2. Add soy sauce, water chestnuts and peppercorns.
3. Cook for 1 minute, tossing water chestnuts.
4. Add lemon juice and blend.
5. Add spinach and toss.
6. Salt to taste and correct seasoning to your taste.
7. Transfer to salad bowl and garnish with chopped egg.

Serves 4.

SALAD DRESSINGS AND SAUCES

This dressing is delicious on a tossed salad or on just plain lettuce.

BLEU CHEESE DRESSING

1 pint mayonnaise
1 pint Durkee Famous Sauce
1/3 cup Worcestershire sauce
1/3 cup chopped onion
3/4 cup oil (vegetable or olive)
1/2 teaspoon garlic salt
3/4 pound bleu cheese

1. Break bleu cheese into small bits and combine with the other ingredients.
2. Mix thoroughly and refrigerate.

Makes about three pints dressing.

If you like richer dressing use cream instead of milk.

RICHARD NEUBECK'S BOILED SALAD DRESSING

2 teaspoons flour
2 egg yolks
3/4 cup milk
1/2 teaspoon vinegar
1/2 teaspoon salt
1 teaspoon prepared mustard
2 tablespoons granulated sugar
1 tablespoon butter, melted

1. Heat the milk in top of a double boiler.
2. In a separate pan, combine the flour and butter and mix thoroughly.
3. Add flour mixture to the milk.
4. Beat in the egg yolks (while cooking).
5. Add the sugar and salt.
6. Add the vinegar and mustard.
7. Continue cooking until the mixture thickens.
8. Remove from heat and thin with a little milk, if necessary.

Makes 1-1/4 cups dressing.

This is an excellent dressing to serve with raw cauliflower.

DIP OR SALAD DRESSING

1 quart mayonnaise
3 cups buttermilk
1 teaspoon monosodium glutamate
1 teaspoon black pepper
1 teaspoon onion salt
1/2 teaspoon garlic salt

1. Mix all ingredients together in a blender.
2. Put in a bottle and refrigerate.
3. Let stand for 24 hours before using. Do not remix.

Makes 7 cups.

From the kitchen of a prize-winning cook.

MARGE STUCKER'S HOMEMADE FRENCH DRESSING

1 cup salad oil
1 cup vinegar
1 cup granulated sugar
3/4 cup catsup
1 garlic clove
1 small onion (chopped fine)
1/4 teaspoon black pepper
1/2 teaspoon paprika
1 teaspoon dry mustard
juice of one lemon
1/2 teaspoon thyme
1/4 teaspoon curry powder
1 teaspoon Dijon mustard (made with white wine)
1 tablespoon Worcestershire sauce

1. Mix all ingredients in blender for one minute.
2. Refrigerate.
Yields 4 cups.

This salad dressing is a little trouble to make, but when you put it on your fruit salad you will say it was worth it.

FRUIT SALAD DRESSING

1/2 cup pineapple juice
1/2 cup water
1/2 cup granulated sugar
grated rind and juice of one lemon
juice of one orange
1 egg, beaten
1 tablespoon butter
4 teaspoons cornstarch
1/2 teaspoon salt
1/2 pint whipping cream, whipped

1. Dissolve cornstarch in orange juice. Set aside.
2. Mix together thoroughly the pineapple juice, water, sugar, rind and juice of lemon, egg, butter and salt.
3. Add orange juice and cornstarch mixture.
4. Bring to a boil over medium heat and boil for two minutes.
5. Remove from heat.
6. When cool add the whipped cream and serve.

Makes two cups dressing.

If you like to make your own salad dressings, this is a quick and easy Italian Dressing to prepare.

ITALIAN DRESSING

1/2 cup olive oil
1/4 cup tarragon vinegar
1/4 teaspoon salt
1/4 teaspoon celery salt
1/4 teaspoon black pepper
1/8 teaspoon garlic powder
1/4 teaspoon onion juice
dash powdered red pepper

1. Place all ingredients in a covered jar or bottle.
2. Shake vigorously to mix thoroughly.
3. Refrigerate until chilled.

Makes 3/4 cup dressing.

If you prefer your own mayonnaise over commercial mayonnaise, this is easy to prepare.

MAYONNAISE

1 egg, beaten
1-1/2 cups olive oil
1 tablespoon vinegar
1 tablespoon lemon juice
1/2 teaspoon salt
1/4 teaspoon prepared mustard
1/4 teaspoon paprika

1. In a blender, mix salt, paprika and mustard.
2. Add vinegar and egg and continue to blend.
3. Add 1/4 of the olive oil and blend until mixture starts to thicken.
4. Continue to add the oil slowly, about 1/4 the amount each time.
5. After all the oil has been added continue to blend until mixture thickens.
6. Add the lemon juice.

Yields about 2 cups.

If you ever serve your guests Chef Salad you will find this is just
the dressing for it.

OUR SALAD DRESSING

1 pint salad dressing
1 pint catsup
1 pint chili sauce
2/3 cup prepared mustard
3/4 cup oil (vegetable or olive)
1/4 cup finely chopped onions
1/2 teaspoon white pepper
1 tablespoon Worcestershire sauce
1/2 teaspoon garlic salt
1/2 cup tarragon vinegar
1/4 teaspoon Tabasco sauce
1 teaspoon red pepper

1. Combine all ingredients and mix thoroughly.
2. Refrigerate.

Makes about four pints dressing.

Mrs. Bob Futrell's Sour Cream Dressing is especially good when served on tossed salad.

SOUR CREAM DRESSING

1 pint sour cream
4 teaspoons sugar
4 tablespoons lemon juice
1/8 teaspoon minced garlic
1 tablespoon milk
1 medium-sized onion (chopped fine)
salt and pepper to taste

1. Mix all ingredients thoroughly.
2. Refrigerate for at least one hour before serving.

Yields one pint dressing.

An excellent dressing for your fruit salads.

SWEET AND SOUR DRESSING

1 cup salad oil
1/4 cup wine vinegar
1/2 cup granulated sugar
1/8 teaspoon salt
1/8 teaspoon dry mustard

1. Mix vinegar, sugar, salt and mustard.
2. In a saucepan bring this mixture to a boil.
3. Let cool.
4. Put in a mixing bowl and slowly add oil while beating until mixture thickens.
5. Refrigerate. Shake before using.

Makes 1-3/4 cups.
This dressing can be refrigerated for several weeks.

This is an excellent dressing for a tossed salad.

VINEGAR AND OIL DRESSING

1/2 cup granulated sugar
1/4 teaspoon salt
1/4 teaspoon black pepper
1/2 cup white vinegar
2 tablespoons vegetable oil

Combine all ingredients and mix well. We find that putting them in a jar and shaking is an excellent way to do this.

Makes one cup dressing.

This is a good standard barbecue sauce.

BARBECUE SAUCE

1/2 cup onions (finely chopped)
1 ounce shortening
1 tablespoon beef soup base
1 cup catsup
2 teaspoons dry mustard
3 tablespoons brown sugar
1/2 cup water
3-1/4 tablespoons wine vinegar
2 teaspoons Worcestershire sauce
1/4 teaspoon Tabasco sauce

1. Cook onions in shortening until lightly browned.
2. Add remaining ingredients, stirring in well.
3. Simmer for 20 minutes.

Yields one pint.

Our favorite.

SOUTHERN STYLE BARBECUE SAUCE

1 pound butter
1 medium-sized onion (minced)
1/2 cup chili sauce
1/2 cup wine vinegar
1/4 cup Worcestershire sauce
1/4 cup A. 1. Sauce
1 teaspoon sweet basil
1/2 teaspoon oregano
1 teaspoon thyme
1/2 teaspoon cayenne pepper
1 teaspoon dry mustard
1/2 teaspoon black pepper
1 cup tomato sauce
1/2 cup honey
1 teaspoon salt
1 cup water

1. Melt butter and set aside to cool slightly.
2. Mix all other ingredients, combining thoroughly.
3. Add melted butter.
4. Simmer for 15 to 20 minutes.

When preparing meat, baste about every 10 minutes with this sauce.

Yields about 2 pints.

Meat drippings, instead of water, will give this sauce an added taste.

BROWN SAUCE

3 tablespoons butter
3 tablespoons flour
1/4 cup chopped onion
1/4 teaspoon salt
1/8 teaspoon black pepper
1 cup water

1. Cook onion in the butter in a cooking pot over medium heat until browned.
2. Combine the flour, salt and pepper and add to the butter and onion.
3. Continue cooking until browned.
4. Add the water gradually.
5. Bring to a boil and cook for 2 or 3 minutes.

Makes 1 cup.

A standard sauce to serve with lamb.

CURRANT MINT SAUCE

1 cup currant jelly
1 tablespoon grated orange rind
1/2 teaspoon lemon juice
3 tablespoons finely chopped fresh mint leaves

1. Whip the currant jelly until smooth.
2. Add the orange rind, lemon juice and mint and mix well.

Makes 8 ounces sauce.

Note: If you cannot get fresh mint, substitute 2 or 3 drops oil of peppermint or 1/2 teaspoon peppermint extract.

This is a good sauce to serve with fish.

EGG SAUCE

2 egg yolks, beaten
2 tablespoons butter
2 tablespoons flour
1/2 teaspoon salt
1/8 teaspoon black pepper
1 cup cream
3 tablespoons lemon juice

1. Melt butter in a skillet and add the flour, salt and black pepper.
2. Add the cream slowly and bring to a boil. Stir constantly.
3. Cook until the mixture thickens.
4. Transfer mixture to top of a double boiler and add the egg yolks.
5. Cook for 2 or 3 minutes over boiling water.
6. Add lemon juice.
7. Remove from fire and serve hot over fish.

Makes just over 1 cup sauce.

This sauce is best prepared just before using.

HOLLANDAISE SAUCE

1 stick butter
2 egg yolks
juice of two lemons
1/4 teaspoon salt
dash red pepper
1/2 cup boiling water

1. Cream butter in top of a double boiler.
2. Add egg yolks one at a time and beat to blend thoroughly.
3. Add lemon juice, salt and red pepper.
4. Slowly add the boiling water and cook over boiling water in a double boiler, stirring constantly, until the mixture thickens.

Makes 1 cup.

Served with garlic bread and a nice garden salad, this makes a fine meal.

ITALIAN MEAT SAUCE FOR PASTA

1 pound ground beef
2 pounds fresh mushrooms (peeled and cut into pieces)
2 quarts canned tomatoes
2 medium-sized onions (sliced)
2 garlic cloves (minced)
4 tablespoons olive oil
1 16-ounce can seasoned tomato sauce
2 teaspoons oregano
1/2 teaspoon thyme
2 bay leaves
2 teaspoons salt
1 teaspoon black pepper
1 teaspoon monosodium glutamate

1. In a large pot brown onions and garlic together in the olive oil.
2. Add ground beef and mushrooms.
3. Cook over medium-high heat until beef is browned.
4. Add tomatoes, tomato sauce, oregano, thyme, bay leaves, salt, pepper and monosodium glutamate.
5. Bring to a boil; turn down to simmer.
6. Simmer uncovered for two hours. Stir occasionally.
7. Serve over hot, cooked spaghetti or other pasta.

Serves 6 to 8.

This sauce can be prepared without the meat, if you prefer.

SPAGHETTI SAUCE

3/4 pound beef (ground)
1/4 cup olive oil
1 medium-sized onion (chopped fine)
1/2 cup water
1/2 teaspoon garlic powder
2 teaspoons oregano
1 teaspoon salt
1/4 teaspoon black pepper
1/4 teaspoon red pepper
1/2 teaspoon granulated sugar
1/2 cup tomato paste
2 cups tomato purée
2 tablespoons Parmesan cheese (grated)
1 tablespoon butter

1. Melt the butter in a skillet and brown beef and onion together. Set aside.
2. In a cooking pot, heat the tomato purée and tomato paste.
3. Add the meat and onion mixture and the olive oil to the tomato mixture.
4. Put in the water, salt, black pepper, red pepper, sugar, garlic powder, oregano, and Parmesan cheese.
5. Simmer for 2 to 2-1/2 hours, stirring occasionally.
6. Serve hot over spaghetti and top with grated Parmesan cheese.

Serves 6 to 8.

Fish always tastes better when you serve it with tartar sauce. This one is quick and easy.

TARTAR SAUCE

1 hard-cooked egg yolk
1 raw egg yolk
1 egg white, beaten dry and stiff
1/3 cup olive oil
1 teaspoon onion juice
1 teaspoon chopped capers
1 teaspoon chopped green olives
1 teaspoon chopped sweet pickle
1/4 teaspoon salt
1/8 teaspoon black pepper
1 teaspoon mustard
1/2 teaspoon vinegar

1. Mash hard-cooked egg yolk until smooth. (Sieve, if necessary)
2. Add raw egg yolk, mustard, salt and pepper.
3. Add olive oil and mix well.
4. Slowly add the vinegar and continue mixing. Fold in the egg white.
5. Add the cooked egg yolk and combine thoroughly.
6. Add onion juice, capers, olives and pickle. Mix completely.

Makes 4 servings.

You will find many uses for this plain tomato sauce.

TOMATO SAUCE

1-1/2 cups stewed tomatoes
2 tablespoons flour
1 slice of onion (chopped)
3 tablespoons butter
1/2 teaspoon granulated sugar
1/4 teaspoon salt
1/8 teaspoon black pepper

1. Cook onion and tomatoes for 20 minutes.
2. Rub through strainer. Set aside.
3. In a separate saucepan melt the butter.
4. Add the flour, sugar, salt and pepper to the butter.
5. Add to the tomatoes and cook for about 5 minutes.

Yields 1-1/2 cups.

By increasing or decreasing the amount of butter and flour you can make this sauce thicker or thinner to suit your taste.

WHITE SAUCE

2 tablespoons butter
2 tablespoons flour
1 cup milk
1/2 teaspoon salt
1/4 teaspoon white pepper

1. Melt butter in a skillet and add flour, salt and pepper.
2. Slowly add the milk and bring to a boil, stirring constantly.
3. Continue cooking until the mixture thickens.
4. Continue cooking for 2 more minutes.

Makes one cup sauce.

ENTREES

INSTRUCTIONS FOR COOKING
A CLAUDIA SANDERS KENTUCKY COUNTRY HAM

1. Carefully clean the ham, either by scrubbing with a stiff brush or coarse cloth, before cooking.
2. Cut off the hock—which can be used for seasoning with beans, etc.
3. Soak the ham for 12 to 14 hours in cold water. Do not cook your ham in this soaking water.

Your ham is now ready for cooking. There are several ways of cooking a country ham—you can either bake it in a large roasting pan or boil it submerged in a large container. If you will carefully follow the instructions either method will prove satisfactory. Regardless of which process you use, please remember to cook your ham very slowly. This prevents excessive shrinkage and also allows the ham to absorb desirable moisture.

TO BAKE THE HAM

This method is preferred by many people as it eliminates the use of a large container.

1. Use a roasting pan large enough to hold the ham.
2. Place a piece of heavy duty aluminum foil, large enough to wrap the ham, in the bottom of the roasting pan. Place the ham on the foil and pour over it one quart of water, 1/2 cup wine vinegar and 2 cups of brown sugar. Fold the foil over the top of the ham and put the top on the roaster.
3. Place in a very slow oven: 275° F. to 300° F.
4. Your cooking time will average from 4 to 6 hours depending on the size of the ham.

5. Your ham is done when:
    A. It feels tender when tested with a fork.
    B. The large bone on the butt end protrudes.
    C. The rind peels off easily.
6. The ham should be allowed to cool in the pan with wrapping intact.
7. When ham is cool, carefully peel off the rind and trim off any excess fat.
8. To glaze the ham, see below.

TO BOIL OR SIMMER THE HAM

1. Place the ham in a large container. Completely cover with fresh cold water. Put on the stove and bring to a boil—then allow to slowly simmer until the ham is tender, or until the large bone in the butt end of the ham becomes loose and protrudes. Your cooking time will average about 25 minutes to the pound. Add water, if necessary, to keep the ham completely covered.
2. Allow the ham to cool in the cooking water. This causes the ham to retain desirable moisture.
3. When ham has cooled, carefully remove the rind and trim any excess fat.
4. To glaze the ham, see below.

HAM GLAZES

1. Make a mix of fine bread crumbs or coarse water-ground corn meal and brown sugar, half and half. Add enough port wine or fruit juice so it will spread over ham. Place ham back in oven and brown at 400° F. until the sugar is bubbly and a crust forms. Decorate to taste.
2. Mix one cup of brown sugar with 3 tablespoons of port wine or fruit juice—spread this mixture over the ham. Decorate to your own taste. Place ham in an oven and bake at 375° F. to 400° F. for 15 or 20 minutes. Ham should be cut and served only after it has cooled to room temperature, never while it is hot.

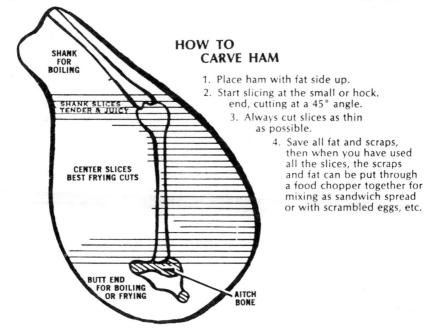

SHANK
FOR
BOILING

SHANK SLICES
TENDER & JUICY

CENTER SLICES
BEST FRYING CUTS

BUTT END
FOR BOILING
OR FRYING

AITCH
BONE

HOW TO CARVE HAM

1. Place ham with fat side up.
2. Start slicing at the small or hock.
   end, cutting at a 45° angle.
3. Always cut slices as thin
   as possible.
4. Save all fat and scraps,
   then when you have used
   all the slices, the scraps
   and fat can be put through
   a food chopper together for
   mixing as sandwich spread
   or with scrambled eggs, etc.

Country Ham is a feature of the Claudia Sanders Dinner House of Shelbyville.

FRIED COUNTRY HAM

1 one-quarter-inch slice Claudia Sanders Kentucky Country Ham

1. Trim off rind and dark, hard edge of slice. Set aside.
2. Trim most of fat from ham and render this fat in a skillet.
3. After all grease has been cooked out of fat, remove the fat from the skillet.
4. Put slice of ham in medium-hot skillet and brown one side. (Caution: cook slowly. Do not let skillet become too hot).
5. Turn ham and brown other side.
6. Repeat until ham is cooked to your taste.

Caution—if cooked too long ham will become hard and dry.

Should the ham be too salty for your taste, you can soak it in water or in milk and sweet syrup for 15 to 30 minutes before cooking.

RED EYE GRAVY
(Make immediately after frying sliced ham)

1. Pour off most of the grease from the skillet.
2. Brown residue in skillet.
3. Add small amount of water or coffee (about 1/4 cup per slice).
To use, spoon over ham, hot biscuits or grits.

CREAM GRAVY

Fix the same as Red Eye Gravy, but use milk or cream instead of water or coffee. If you prefer a thicker gravy, add a little flour and water mixture.

Using Country Ham gives a rich flavor to this ham salad.

COUNTRY HAM SALAD

2 pounds ground, baked Claudia Sanders Kentucky Country Ham
2 cups chopped celery
1 cup Durkee's Famous Sauce
1 cup mayonnaise
1 cup chopped, hard cooked eggs
1 cup green sweet relish

1. Mix ham, celery, eggs and relish together thoroughly.
2. Add the Durkee's Famous Sauce and the mayonnaise, and mix well.

Serves 4 to 6.

This is a good one-course meal for a hungry family.

BEEF CASSEROLE

2 pounds beef round
5 medium-sized white potatoes (peeled and cut into small cubes)
2 large onions (diced)
3/4 cup carrots (cut into small pieces)
3 medium-sized tomatoes (cut into small pieces)
3 tablespoons flour
1 cup canned lima beans
1 teaspoon salt
1 teaspoon black pepper
2 cups water

1. Preheat oven to 300° F.
2. Cut beef into 1-inch cubes.
3. In a greased skillet, brown the beef and onions for about 5 minutes.
4. Mix the flour with 1/4 cup of the water. Set aside.
5. Place the potatoes, carrots, tomatoes and lima beans in a casserole.
6. Add the rest of the water.
7. Add the meat and onions.
8. Stir in the flour and season with the salt and pepper.
9. Bake at 300° F. for 2 to 2-1/2 hours.

Serves 4 to 6.

From the kitchen of Johanna Kohnhorst comes this recipe. It's nothing fancy, but always welcome to a hungry family.

BEEF STEW

3 pounds beef (round is good)
5 white potatoes (peeled and diced)
1 medium-sized onion (diced)
6 carrots (scraped and cut into small pieces)
1 cup peas (fresh or canned)
2 teaspoons salt
1/4 teaspoon black pepper
3 cups boiling water

1. Preheat oven to 500° F.
2. Cut beef into small stewing-size pieces.
3. Sear at 500° F. for about 20 minutes in casserole.
4. Add potatoes, onion, carrots, peas, salt, pepper and boiling water to the meat.
5. Bake at 275° F. in covered casserole for 2-1/2 to 3 hours.

Serves 6 or 7.

A spicy dish!

GROUND BEEF AND RICE CASSEROLE

1 pound ground beef
2 large onions (sliced)
1 quart canned tomatoes with juice
1/3 cup packaged precooked rice
1 medium-sized green pepper (seeded and chopped)
1 teaspoon granulated sugar
1 teaspoon chili powder
1 teaspoon salt
1/8 teaspoon black pepper

1. Preheat oven to 350° F.
2. Fry beef, onions and green pepper over medium heat in a large Corningware casserole until beef is browned.
3. Add tomatoes with juice, rice, sugar, chili powder, salt and pepper. Stir to mix.
4. Bake at 350° F. for one hour.

Serves 4.

Cabbage with an Italian flavor.

CABBAGE ROLLS

6 large cabbage leaves
1 pound coarse-ground beef
1 medium-sized onion
1 teaspoon salt
1/4 teaspoon black pepper
juice of one lemon
1/3 cup plus 6 tablespoons pizza sauce

1. Preheat oven to 350° F.
2. Boil cabbage leaves in salted water for five minutes.
3. Remove leaves and set aside.
4. Grind beef and onion together in food grinder.
5. Brown beef and onion in a large skillet over medium-to-high heat.
6. Add salt and pepper to beef and onion mixture.
7. Add the lemon juice and 1/3 cup of the pizza sauce, stirring constantly.
8. Remove from heat.
9. Place two heaping tablespoons of beef mixture on each cabbage leaf.
10. Fold left and right side of cabbage leaf over the meat and then roll up from bottom to top enclosing meat entirely. Secure with a toothpick if necessary.
11. Place folded leaves in a baking dish and cover each with one tablespoon of the remaining pizza sauce.
12. Bake at 350° F. for 30 minutes.

Makes 6 cabbage rolls.

Sue Heinz tells us this recipe has been in her family for generations.

CHICKEN IN A BAG

1 chicken, cut up as for frying
1 cup Special Sauce, see below

1. Preheat oven to 400° F.
2. Put some of the sauce on a flat dish and roll each piece of chicken in it to cover well.
3. Place chicken pieces on a large piece of foil.
4. Pour remaining sauce over chicken.
5. Fold foil and close over the chicken like a bag.
6. Place foil "bag" on a baking tray or in a large baking dish.
7. Bake at 400° F. for 15 minutes.
8. Lower heat to 350° F. and continue to bake for another hour and 15 minutes.

Serves 2 to 4.

SPECIAL SAUCE

3 tablespoons catsup
2 tablespoons vinegar
1 tablespoon lemon juice
2 tablespoons Worcestershire sauce
4 tablespoons water
1 teaspoon salt
1 teaspoon dry mustard
1 teaspoon chili powder
1 teaspoon paprika
1/2 teaspoon cayenne pepper
3 tablespoons brown sugar
2 tablespoons butter

1. Combine all ingredients in a large bowl and mix thoroughly.
2. Use as directed above.

Makes enough sauce for one chicken.

A good way to prepare an inexpensive main dish.

CHINESE CHICKEN

1 chicken (cut up)
1/2 cup butter
1 cup water chestnuts (diced)
1 cup bamboo shoots
1 cup Chinese pea pods
2 cups diced celery
2 cups cut green beans
3 cups chicken broth
1/4 cup soy sauce
2-1/2 teaspoons salt
2 teaspoons monosodium glutamate
1 teaspoon granulated sugar
1 teaspoon black pepper
2 tablespoons cornstarch
1/2 cup water
2 cups hot cooked rice

1. Skin and slice chicken.
2. Brown in skillet in the 1/2 cup butter.
3. Add water chestnuts, bamboo shoots, pea pods, celery and green beans.
4. Pour in the chicken broth.
5. Add soy sauce, monosodium glutamate, sugar, salt and pepper.
6. Cover and steam for 5 minutes.
7. In a separate dish, blend the cornstarch and water.
8. Add to chicken.
9. Cook over medium heat until liquid is transparent.
10. Serve over hot cooked rice.

Serves 4.

This tasty dish is ideal to serve your company.

CHICKEN WITH SHERRY AND ARTICHOKES

4 pounds chicken (cut into frying pieces)
1/2 cup butter
1 cup flour
2 teaspoons salt
1 teaspoon pepper
1-1/2 cups cooking sherry
2 16 oz. cans artichoke hearts, drained
1 pound fresh mushrooms (sliced 1/4-inch thick)

1. Preheat oven to 350° F.
2. Wash chicken and pat dry with paper towel.
3. Sift flour, salt and pepper together and put in a bag.
4. Shake chicken in the flour mixture covering each piece well.
5. In a large pan, or skillet, melt the butter.
6. Brown the chicken pieces in the butter over medium heat.
7. Cover bottom of a large casserole with half the chicken. Add one can of artichokes and 1/2 the mushrooms.
8. Add remaining chicken and cover with the rest of the artichokes and mushrooms.
9. Pour sherry in the skillet in which you browned the chicken and dislodge any brownings which may have stuck to the skillet.
10. Pour this over the chicken.
11. Bake at 350° F. for 45 minutes.

Serves 8.

A lot of people have told me this is the best chili they have ever eaten. Be sure to add the chili powder *before* you put in the tomatoes, beans and chili mix.

CHERRY SETTLE'S CHILI

1 pound ground beef
1 8-oz. carton prepared chili mix *or* 1 8-oz. can prepared chili
2 medium-sized onions (chopped)
2 tablespoons chili powder
2 quarts tomatoes (canned or fresh cooked)
1 16-oz. can red kidney beans in chili gravy
1 teaspoon salt

1. In a large cooking pot cook the onions and ground beef together until browned.
2. Add chili powder and mix well.
3. Add tomatoes, chili mix, kidney beans and salt.
4. Bring to a boil.
5. Turn down to simmer and simmer for one hour.
6. Serve in a bowl with 1/2 to 1 cup cooked spaghetti.

Makes four quarts.

While we like it this way, it might make you feel more Oriental if you added 1/2 cup bamboo shoots to this recipe. If you do, cut them in small pieces.

CHOP SUEY

1 pound fresh veal
1/2 cup onions, sliced thin
1/2 cup celery, cut crosswise in thin slices
1 green pepper (seeds removed and sliced thin)
1 cup chopped mushrooms
1 cup bean sprouts
1/4 cup rice
1 teaspoon salt
1/8 teaspoon black pepper
1 teaspoon soy sauce
2 tablespoons butter
3 cups water

1. Boil veal in salted water until done.
2. Drain, cool and cut into short, thin slices.
3. Brown veal together with the onions in 1/2 the butter in a skillet. Set aside.
4. Preheat oven to 350° F.
5. Put the water in a baking dish and add the celery, green pepper, mushrooms, bean sprouts, rice, salt, soy sauce, black pepper and the rest of the butter.
6. Put in the meat and onions.
7. Bake at 350° F. for about 1-1/4 hours.

Serves 6 to 8.

The Claudia Sanders Dinner House uses nothing but Marion-Kay spices in all its recipes.

FRIED CHICKEN

1 frying chicken, cut into frying pieces
1 cup flour
2 eggs, well beaten
2/3 cup milk
1-1/2 tablespoons Claudia Sanders Chicken seasoning. (Marion-Kay Company)
enough vegetable oil, or shortening, to cover bottom of your skillet about 1/8 inch.

1. Combine eggs and milk. Set aside.
2. Combine flour with the 1-1/2 tablespoon Claudia Sanders Chicken Seasoning.
3. Dip chicken pieces in milk-egg mixture and roll them in the flour-seasoning mixture.
4. Fry pieces in low to medium heat for 15 to 20 minutes, turning once.
5. Remove from fire. Drain and serve.

Serves 2 to 4.

Claudia Sanders Chicken Seasoning is available in Gourmet shops, local markets, or dealers. It may be purchased by mail from the Marion-Kay Company, Brownstown, Indiana 47220.
To order by mail send $2.00 for family size package plus $1.00 postage.

A perfect way to use leftover ham.

HAM TETRAZZINI

8-ounce box spaghetti (broken into 2-inch pieces)
1 can cream of mushroom soup
1 cup milk
1 small onion (chopped)
1 cup sharp cheese (shredded)
1/2 teaspoon salt
1/8 teaspoon black pepper
1 teaspoon Worcestershire sauce
1/8 cup chopped pimiento
2 cups diced baked ham
1/4 cup Parmesan cheese (grated)

1. Preheat oven to 375° F.
2. Cook spaghetti in salted water until tender.
3. Drain spaghetti and set aside.
4. In a saucepan, combine the cream of mushroom soup, milk, onion, sharp cheese, salt, pepper, pimiento and Worcestershire sauce.
5. Pour over spaghetti and toss lightly.
6. In a buttered casserole arrange a layer of spaghetti, then a layer of ham, a layer of spaghetti, then ham until you have used all the spaghetti and ham.
7. Top with the grated Parmesan cheese.
8. Bake at 375° for 20 minutes or until hot and bubbly.

Serves 4 to 6.

When your brave hunter brings home the game, make him feel proud by preparing the rabbit this way.

HASENPFEFFER

1 2-1/2 pound rabbit (cut into frying pieces)
2-1/2 tablespoons salt
6 tablespoons butter
1 medium-sized onion
4 whole cloves
1 cup port wine
1/4 cup lemon juice
12 whole peppercorns
1 sprig parsley
1/2 teaspoon thyme
1 bay leaf
2 cans beef bouillon
3 tablespoons flour

1. Preheat oven to 350° F.
2. Rinse rabbit in cold water and pat dry with paper towel.
3. Rub with 1-1/2 tablespoons of the salt.
4. In a hot skillet, melt 3 tablespoons of the butter.
5. Brown rabbit on all sides (about 20 minutes).
6. When browned, place in a 3-quart casserole.
7. Put in the onion stuck with the four whole cloves.
8. Add wine, lemon juice, peppercorns, parsley, thyme, bay leaf, bouillon and the rest of the salt.
9. Bake at 350° F. in covered casserole for 1-1/2 hours.
10. Remove from oven and discard the onion.
11. Put rabbit in the serving dish and cover with the following sauce:

SAUCE

1. Melt the remaining butter in a saucepan.
2. Add the flour and stir while cooking until smooth.
3. Add the broth from the rabbit.
4. Bring to a boil, stirring constantly. Continue cooking until gravy becomes thick.
5. Use as directed.

Serves 6.

This is the Claudia Sanders Dinner House of Shelbyville version of the famous Hot Brown sandwich.

HOT BROWN

1-1/2 cups cheese sauce (see page 85)
1 slice white toast
1 slice white meat of turkey
1 slice Claudia Sanders Kentucky Country Ham
2 slices cooked bacon
1/4 cup grated sharp cheese
1/4 cup grated Parmesan cheese
1 peach half (canned)
paprika to garnish

1. Preheat oven to 400° F.
2. Put 2 tablespoons cheese sauce on bottom of an individual baking dish.
3. Place the toast on this sauce.
4. Cover the toast with 3 tablespoons cheese sauce.
5. Put layer of ham over this.
6. Cover with 3 tablespoons cheese sauce.
7. Sprinkle 1/2 the Parmesan cheese on this layer of cheese sauce and put on the slice of white meat of turkey.
8. Cover with 3 tablespoons cheese sauce.
9. Sprinkle the grated sharp cheese over this.
10. Sprinkle on the rest of the Parmesan cheese and place peach half in center of the sandwich.
11. Garnish with paprika.
12. Place one slice bacon at each side of the peach half.
13. Bake at 400° F. for 15 minutes.
14. Serve in baking dish while hot.

Makes one sandwich.

CHEESE SAUCE FOR HOT BROWN

2 tablespoons margarine
2 tablespoons all-purpose flour
1 cup milk
1 cup shredded Cheddar cheese
1/4 teaspoon salt
dash white pepper

1. Melt margarine in saucepan over low heat.
2. Blend in the flour, salt and white pepper.
3. Add milk slowly, stirring as you add it.
4. Put in the shredded cheese and continue to cook and stir until the cheese has completely melted.

Makes 1-1/2 cups sauce (enough for one sandwich).

This is a popular family dish. It can be prepared ahead of time and baked at the last minute.

LASAGNE

2 4-ounce packages pizza cheese (shredded)
1 pound ground beef
2 8-ounce cans tomato sauce
2 tablespoons butter
1/4 teaspoon salt
1 8-ounce package broad lasagne noodles
1 cup cottage cheese
2 teaspoons garlic salt
1/2 teaspoon black pepper

1. Preheat oven to 350° F.
2. Brown ground beef in butter.
3. Stir in tomato sauce, salt, pepper and garlic salt. Set aside.
4. Cook noodles in boiling salt water for 10 minutes.
5. Drain noodles and rinse in cold water.
6. In buttered baking dish put a layer of noodles.
7. Add a layer of pizza cheese; then a layer of noodles.
8. Add another layer of pizza cheese.
9. Add a layer of noodles mixed with the cottage cheese.
10. Top with ground beef mixture.
11. Bake at 350° F. for 45 minutes.
12. Cut in squares and serve.

Serves about 8.

Serve this with hot garlic bread and a tossed salad with Italian dressing.

LOBSTER CHERRY SETTLE

4 South African lobster tails (frozen)

SAUCE

1/3 cup olive oil
1 quart canned tomatoes (we like home-canned)
2 cloves garlic, chopped fine
2 teaspoons oregano
1/2 teaspoon salt
1/4 teaspoon black pepper
a pinch of red pepper pod

TO PREPARE FROZEN LOBSTER TAILS

1. Thaw lobster tails quickly. (Just enough to separate pieces.)
2. Open rear end of tail to resemble a fan.
3. Bend the fan upward to break so that it will stay open.
4. With kitchen scissors cut down the center of the hard-shell back of the tail to the fan end.
5. Spread shell open to expose lobster meat.
6. With fingers, pull meat out of the shell and lay on top of the shell.
7. Put the four lobster tails in a baking dish and set aside.

TO PREPARE SAUCE AND COOK THE LOBSTER TAILS

1. Preheat oven to 350° F.
2. Heat olive oil in a large skillet over medium heat.
3. Add chopped garlic cloves and sauté for about two minutes.
4. Add tomatoes, pinch of pepper pod, oregano, salt and pepper.
5. Continue cooking over medium heat for 10 minutes, stirring occasionally.
6. Spoon sauce over prepared lobster tails.
7. Bake at 350° F. for about 30 minutes.

Serves 2.

Claudia Stivers says her family and guests always ask for a second helping when she serves her meat loaf.

MEAT LOAF WITH SAUCE

1-1/2 pounds ground beef
2/3 cup dry bread crumbs
1 cup milk
2 eggs, beaten
1/2 cup tomato sauce
1/4 cup grated onion
1 teaspoon salt
1/8 teaspoon black pepper
1/2 teaspoon sage

1. Preheat oven to 350° F.
2. In a large bowl, soak the bread crumbs in the milk.
3. Add beef, eggs, tomato sauce, onion, salt, pepper and sage and mix well.
4. Form into a single loaf and place in baking pan.
5. Cover with sauce below.
6. Bake at 350° F. for one hour.

Serves 4 to 6.

SAUCE FOR MEAT LOAF

4 ounces tomato sauce
1/2 cup water
3 tablespoons vinegar
3 tablespoons brown sugar
2 tablespoons dry mustard
2 teaspoons Worcestershire sauce

1. Combine all ingredients, mixing thoroughly.
2. Pour over meat loaf, basting one or two times during the cooking.

Prepare mushrooms this simple way when you have that one special friend over for luncheon.

MUSHROOMS ON TOAST

1 cup canned mushroom caps (drained)
4 tablespoons water
3 tablespoons butter
1/4 teaspoon salt
1/8 teaspoon black pepper
2 slices toasted white bread brushed with melted butter.

1. Heat the 4 tablespoons water in a skillet.
2. Add and melt the 3 tablespoons butter.
3. Season with the salt and pepper and mix thoroughly.
4. Add the mushroom caps.
5. Fry over moderate heat for about 5 minutes. Stir often.
6. Place caps on the buttered toast and pour any remaining liquid from the skillet over them.

Makes 2 generous servings.

Our variation of a very old recipe.

PEPPER STEAK

1-1/2 lbs. round steak, cut into strips 2-inches long and 1/2 inch thick
1/4 cup flour (unsifted)
1/2 teaspoon salt
1/8 teaspoon black pepper
1/4 cup cooking oil
1 cup canned tomatoes
1-3/4 cups water
1/2 cup chopped onion
1 small garlic clove, minced
1-1/2 teaspoons Worcestershire sauce
2 large green peppers cut in strips
hot cooked rice

1. Combine flour, salt and pepper and coat meat strips with this.
2. In a large skillet cook meat in hot oil until brown on all sides.
3. Drain the tomatoes; save the liquid.
4. Add tomato liquid, water, onion, and garlic to meat in skillet.
5. Cover and simmer about 1-1/4 hours or until meat is tender.
6. Uncover and stir in Worcestershire sauce while still cooking.
7. Add green pepper strips. Replace cover and simmer for 5 minutes.
8. If necessary, thicken gravy with a mixture of a little flour and cold water.
9. Add drained tomatoes and cook for another 5 minutes.
10. Serve over hot rice.

Serves 6.

In the summer when the green peppers are plentiful, try this interesting way to use them.

PEPPER STEAK MY WAY

3 pounds prime steak, cut into strips 2-inches long and 1/2-inch thick
1 pound green peppers, cut into strips
1/4 cup olive oil
2 cups celery, sliced thin and diagonally
1 pound fresh mushrooms, sliced
4 fresh tomatoes, peeled and quartered
1 can chicken broth
1 teaspoon salt
1/2 teaspoon black pepper
1/4 teaspoon monosodium glutamate
1/2 cup soy sauce
1 tablespoon cornstarch
hot cooked rice

1. In a large skillet, brown steak in olive oil.
2. Add salt, pepper and monosodium glutamate.
3. Add green peppers, celery and mushrooms and cook for another 2 minutes.
4. Add chicken broth and fresh tomatoes and continue cooking for another 5 minutes.
5. Turn heat to medium and add soy sauce combined with the cornstarch. Stir constantly until sauce thickens.
6. We recommend this be served over hot rice.

Serves 8.

The pineapple adds a special flavor to the pork chops.

PINEAPPLE PORK CHOPS

4 center-cut pork chops
1 teaspoon salt
1/2 teaspoon black pepper
1 small can pineapple slices (save the juice)
1/2 teaspoon ground cloves
1 tablespoon cornstarch

1. Trim fat from chops.
2. Render the fat in a hot skillet.
3. Discard the fat and brown the chops on both sides.
4. Season with the salt and pepper.
5. Add enough water to pineapple juice to make 1 cup liquid.
6. Add this and the cloves to the pork chops.
7. Bring to a boil and turn down to simmer.
8. Simmer for one hour, covered.
9. Add pineapple to chops and continue simmering until heated thoroughly.
10. Remove pork chops and pineapple from skillet and place on a serving platter.
11. In a cup mix the cornstarch with a little water and stir this into the skillet to make gravy.
12. Pour gravy over pork chops and serve.

Serves 4.

Take a culinary trip down South with pork and sweet 'taters.

PORK WITH SWEET POTATOES

1 2-pound pork tenderloin
4 or 5 medium-sized sweet potatoes
1 teaspoon salt
1/4 teaspoon black pepper
2/3 cup water, apple juice, or white wine

1. Preheat oven to 500° F.
2. Wipe pork tenderloin and rub with salt and pepper.
3. Sear in 500° F. oven for about 15 minutes on rack in open roasting pan.
4. Parboil sweet potatoes for 15 or 20 minutes; peel, cut into slices lengthwise and place in roasting pan around tenderloin.
5. Reduce heat to 350° F. and add 2/3 cup of water, apple juice, or wine.
6. Roast for one hour or until done. Baste four or five times during roasting.

Serves 4 or 5.

Little mess and a meal that's really filling.

POT ROAST

1 3-4-pound pot roast
1 package onion soup mix
1 cup water
4 potatoes, peeled and cut in half
4 carrots, peeled and cut into strips
salt and pepper to taste

1. Preheat oven to 350° F.
2. Place all ingredients in a casserole.
3. Bake at 350° F., covered, for one hour.

Serves 6 to 8.

Don't forget Yorkshire Pudding when you serve roast beef.

ROAST BEEF

1 6-pound roast
3 teaspoons salt (1/2 teaspoon per pound)
1/2 teaspoon black pepper
flour

1. Preheat oven to 500° F.
2. Wipe roast.
3. Rub with the salt and pepper.
4. Dredge meat and roasting pan with flour.
5. Place roast fat side up on rack in roasting pan. (If roast is lean, fasten some suet on top with skewers. Otherwise, baste the roast occasionally.)
6. Place in 500° F. oven for about 20 minutes, or until flour in pan browns.
7. Reduce heat to 300° F.
8. Cook as follows:

15 minutes to the pound for rare.
20 minutes to the pound for medium rare.
30 minutes to the pound for well-done.
Serves 10.

We like to serve this with Currant Mint sauce, page 60.

ROAST LEG OF LAMB

4 pound leg of lamb
3 or 4 strips bacon
1-1/2 teaspoons salt
1/4 teaspoon black pepper
1-1/2 tablespoons flour

1. Preheat oven to 450° F.
2. Wipe leg of lamb and rub with salt, pepper and flour.
3. Place on rack in uncovered roasting pan cut side up.
4. Roast at 450° F. for 30 minutes.
5. Reduce heat to 300° F. and lay bacon strips across lamb.
6. Roast for another 2 to 2-1/2 hours, or until done.

Serves 8 to 10.

Salisbury Steak is always a delicious way to prepare and serve hamburger.

SALISBURY STEAK

2 pounds hamburger
1 egg, beaten
1/4 cup cold water
1/4 cup chopped onion
3 tablespoons sweet relish
1 teaspoon Worcestershire sauce
1 tablespoon salt
1 teaspoon black pepper
1 slice white bread, toasted and chopped fine

1. Combine the hamburger, onion, relish and toast.
2. Add egg and mix thoroughly.
3. Season with the salt, black pepper and Worcestershire sauce.
4. Add the water.
5. Make into patties and broil for 20 minutes or until done.

Serves 4.

This is easy to prepare and is attractive when garnished with paprika and chopped parsley.

BAKED TOMATOES STUFFED WITH MUSHROOMS

6 medium-sized tomatoes
1/2 cup bread crumbs
1/4 teaspoon salt
1/8 teaspoon black pepper
1/2 teaspoon finely chopped onion
2/3 cup finely chopped mushrooms

1. Preheat oven to 400° F.
2. Wash tomatoes and cut slice from stem end.
3. Scoop out seeds and pulp.
4. Mix the bread crumbs, salt, pepper, onion and mushrooms and add to the pulp.
5. Stuff the tomatoes with this mixture.
6. Bake at 400° F. for about 20 minutes in buttered pan.

Serves 6.

For variety, when you make this you can add 1/2 onion chopped fine.

VEAL LOAF

1-1/2 pounds ground veal
1 egg, beaten
4 tablespoons cracker crumbs
1 teaspoon salt
3 tablespoons chopped parsley
1/4 teaspoon black pepper
1/4 teaspoon sage
1/4 cup milk
2 tablespoons melted butter

1. Preheat oven to 400° F.
2. Combine the egg, cracker crumbs, salt, parsley, black pepper, sage and milk in a large bowl.
3. Work in the ground veal, mixing all the ingredients thoroughly.
4. Place in a well-greased loaf pan.
5. Brush top of loaf with the melted butter.
6. Bake at 400° F. for 45 to 50 minutes.

Serves 5 or 6.

A one-dish meal. Just add a nice tossed green salad and hot bread and you've "got it made."

YUMMY CHICKEN

1/4 cup olive oil
1 frying chicken (cut up)
1 can cream of chicken soup (10-3/4 ounce)
3/4 cup milk
1/2 teaspoon thyme
1/2 teaspoon salt
1/4 teaspoon black pepper
1/4 teaspoon monosodium glutamate
1 dozen spring onions (tops cut off: Just use onions)
1 10-ounce package frozen peas
1 stalk celery (finely sliced)
4 carrots (finely sliced)

1. Preheat oven to 350° F.
2. In a heavy iron skillet brown chicken pieces in the olive oil.
3. Remove chicken and place in a 3-quart casserole. Set aside.
4. In the skillet, blend chicken soup with the milk, stirring to scrape bottom of skillet to get brownings.
5. Add onions, peas, carrots, celery, thyme, salt, pepper and monosodium glutamate to the soup mixture and cook over medium heat for 10 minutes.
6. Pour soup mixture over chicken in casserole.
7. Bake at 350° F., covered, for 1 hour.

Serves 6

Quick, easy to prepare and mighty satisfying!

WELSH RAREBIT

1/4 cup milk
6 1-ounce slices American cheese
1 tablespoon Worcestershire sauce
2 tablespoons prepared mustard
1/4 teaspoon salt
1/8 teaspoon black pepper
saltine crackers or toast points

1. Heat the milk in a saucepan.
2. Add the cheese. Cook until cheese is completely melted.
3. Add the Worcestershire sauce, mustard, salt and pepper and blend well.
4. Serve over saltines or toast trimmed of crusts, while rarebit is hot.

Serves 2.

VEGETABLES

This is a real taste-pleaser at the Dinner House.

BAKED APPLES

5 to 6 cups canned apples in their own juice
3/4 cup white sugar
3/4 cup light brown sugar
1 cup Clearjel
1 stick butter
cinnamon to taste

1. Preheat oven to 325° F.
2. Stir all dry ingredients together.
3. Mix in apples.
4. Dot with butter.
5. Bake at 325°F. until apples are tender.

Serves 12.

Green beans are one of the famous eight vegetables served with each dinner at the Claudia Sanders Dinner House of Shelbyville.

GREEN BEANS

1 quart canned green beans
4 strips bacon, cut into small pieces
1 tablespoon fine-chopped onion
1/2 teaspoon salt
1/4 teaspoon black pepper

1. Drain liquid off beans. Save liquid. Set beans aside.
2. To the liquid add bacon pieces, onion, salt and pepper.
3. Cook over medium heat until onion is clear and tender.
4. Add beans and heat thoroughly.

Serves 4 to 5.

My family claims these are the best green beans in the world.

CHERRY SETTLE'S STYLE DILLED GREEN BEANS

2 quarts canned green beans (I use my own home-canned)
1/2 pound Claudia Sanders Country Bacon (diced)
1 large onion (sliced very thin)
1 tablespoon salt
1 tablespoon dill weed

1. In a large pot with a lid that will close very tightly, alternate a layer of green beans, onion, bacon.
2. After each layer, sprinkle with salt and dill weed.
3. Add just enough water to keep beans from sticking.
4. Bring to a boil. Cover.
5. Turn down flame to simmer for at least one hour.

Serves 8 to 10.

Here is a delicious green bean recipe that's fast and easy to fix.

GREEN BEANS WITH SOUR CREAM

1 cup sliced mushrooms
2 tablespoons fat
4 cups cooked green beans
1 cup sour cream
1/4 teaspoon salt
1/8 teaspoon black pepper

1. Brown mushrooms in fat in a skillet over medium heat.
2. Add green beans, sour cream, salt and pepper.
3. Continue cooking over medium heat until thoroughly heated.

Serves 6.

You must be sure to use tiny, or rose bud, beets when preparing this dish which is one of the favorites at the Claudia Sanders Dinner House of Shelbyville.

HARVARD BEETS

1 quart canned tiny beets (rose bud when available)
1 tablespoon white vinegar
1 teaspoon salt
1/4 cup fresh orange juice
1/2 cup granulated sugar
1-1/2 tablespoons cornstarch

1. Drain beets. Set aside. Save the juice.
2. Mix cornstarch into a small amount of the juice. Set aside.
3. Add vinegar, salt and orange juice to the rest of the beet juice.
4. Cook over medium heat until mixture comes to a boil and boil for one or two minutes.
5. Put in the cornstarch mixture and continue cooking until mixture thickens.
6. Add the sugar and cook until sugar dissolves.
7. Add beets and cook until heated thoroughly.

Serves 6.
If you wish, you may add 1 teaspoon red coloring while cooking beets.

The chances are you will be asked for this dish over and over again.

SWEET RED CABBAGE

1 pound cooked red cabbage, shredded
1 small apple (grated)
1 small onion (diced)
1/4 pound bacon (chopped)
1/2 cup peach juice
1 bay leaf
1/4 teaspoon allspice
2 cloves
1 tablespoon raw white potato (finely grated)

1. Fry the chopped bacon until slightly brown.
2. Add diced onion and grated apple.
3. Cook for another five minutes.
4. Add all other ingredients and simmer for 20 minutes. (The raw potato will thicken the mixture)

Serves 6.

This recipe adds a tangy flavor to plain cabbage.

SWEET-AND-SOUR CABBAGE

1 small head cabbage, shredded
1/2 pound chopped bacon
2-1/2 cups water
1/3 cup vinegar
1 small-sized onion (diced)
2 tablespoons brown sugar
2 tablespoons flour
1/4 teaspoon sweet basil
1/2 teaspoon salt
1/4 teaspoon black pepper

1. Place 2 cups of water in a cooking pot and bring to a rapid boil.
2. Add cabbage and salt.
3. Cook for 5 minutes; drain and set aside.
4. In a skillet slightly brown the bacon; add onion and continue cooking for 5 minutes.
5. Mix flour and sugar and add to bacon and onion mixture; cook for one minute.
6. Place this mixture together with the vinegar, the rest of the water, sweet basil, pepper, and the cabbage and simmer for about 10 minutes.

Serves 6 to 8.

Kitty Willet says that even men and children will like carrots cooked her way.

CARROT CASSEROLE

2 cups carrots (cooked and mashed)
1/2 stick butter
1/2 cup milk
2 eggs, beaten
2 cups grated Cheddar cheese
1/2 teaspoon salt
1/8 teaspoon black pepper

1. Preheat oven to 350° F.
2. Combine butter, milk, eggs and carrots. Mix well.
3. Season with the salt and pepper.
4. Put the cheese in loosely.
5. Bake at 350° F. for 20 minutes in an ungreased casserole.
6. Remove and sprinkle with topping (recipe below).
7. Bake at 350° F. for another 15 minutes.

Serves 6.

TOPPING FOR CARROT CASSEROLE

1/3 cup melted butter
18 butter crackers (crushed)
1/2 cup chopped pecans

Mix all ingredients until crackers are well coated.

If rabbits could cook, we think this is the way they would cook carrots. If your children balk at eating carrots, try this.

CANDIED CARROTS

6 or 8 medium-sized carrots
1/2 cup maple syrup
1/4 cup water
3/4 cup brown sugar
4 tablespoons butter or corn oil margarine
1/4 teaspoon cinnamon

1. Boil carrots in salted water for about 25 minutes.
2. Scrape and cut into small strips. Set aside.
3. In a baking dish, mix the maple syrup, water, sugar, butter and cinnamon.
4. Add the carrots.
5. Bake in preheated 350° F. oven for 25 to 30 minutes, or until candied.

Serves 6 to 8.

For this dish to be really successful be sure your carrots are ground to a smooth consistency.

CARROT SOUFFLÉ

6 to 8 carrots
1 cup milk
1 tablespoon regular flour
1 tablespoon brown sugar
1 tablespoon granulated sugar
1/2 teaspoon salt
1 egg, well beaten
1 tablespoon melted butter

1. Clean, scrape and cut carrots into small pieces.
2. Boil in salted water for about 25 minutes or until carrots are soft.
3. Grind carrots in food grinder until smooth.
4. In separate dish combine egg, milk and flour.
5. Add salt, sugars and melted butter.
6. Stir in carrots, mixing thoroughly.
7. Bake in preheated 325° F. oven for 30 minutes in buttered baking dish.

Serves 6.

This is an easy party dish that can be prepared ahead of time, refrigerated, and baked at the last minute.

SCALLOPED CAULIFLOWER

1 10-1/2-ounce can condensed cream of celery soup
2 beaten eggs
1/2 cup shredded sharp Cheddar cheese
1/2 cup bread crumbs
1/4 cup snipped parsley
1/4 cup chopped canned pimientos
1 tablespoon minced onion
1/2 teaspoon salt
pepper—just a dash
2 9-ounce packages frozen cauliflower (thawed)

1. Preheat oven to 370° F.
2. Mix all ingredients.
3. Place in 10x6x1-1/2-inch baking dish.
4. Bake at 370° for 45 minutes.

Serves 6 to 8.

The customers at the Claudia Sanders Dinner House think corn pudding an excellent dish with beef or chicken.

CORN PUDDING

2 cups frozen corn
2 eggs, well beaten
1-1/4 cups half & half
3 tablespoons flour
3 tablespoons butter
2 tablespoons sugar
1 teaspoon salt
1/8 teaspoon black pepper

1. Preheat oven to 375° F.
2. Melt butter in a saucepan.
3. Stir in flour, sugar, salt and pepper.
4. Slowly add half & half.
5. Stir in corn.
6. Fold in eggs.
7. Pour into a well buttered 1-quart casserole.
8. Set casserole in pan of hot water.
9. Bake at 375° F. for 15 minutes.
10. Lower temperature to 350° F. and continue baking until set (about 30 minutes).

Serves 6.

The Claudia Sanders Dinner House of Shelbyville serves eggplant as "Mock Oysters".

EGGPLANT CASSEROLE

4 cups eggplant, peeled and cut into small pieces (about 1/2-inch cubes, soaked overnight in salted water)
   1 stick butter
   1 pint half-and-half (approx.)
   1 teaspoon salt
   1/2 teaspoon black pepper
   1 box saltines (broken into crumbs)

1.   Remove eggplant pieces from the water they have soaked in overnight.
2.   In a cooking pot, cover eggplant with fresh, slightly salted water and cook over medium heat for about 20 minutes, or until eggplant is tender.
3.   Drain in a colander. Set aside.
4.   Preheat oven to 350° F.
5.   Line bottom of casserole with saltine crumbs.
6.   Cover with 2 cups of the eggplant.
7.   Season with half the salt and pepper.
8.   Cut half the butter into small pieces and sprinkle over the top of the eggplant.
9.   Cover this with a layer of saltine crumbs.
10. Add the remaining two cups eggplant.
11. Season with the rest of the salt and pepper.
12. Cover top with saltine crumbs; cut remaining butter into small pieces and sprinkle over top of crumbs.
13. Pour in enough half-and-half to cover.
14. Bake at 350° F. for one hour, or until top layer browns.

Serves 8.

A new way to fix a Southern vegetable.

SWEET-AND-SOUR OKRA

1 pound small, fresh okra
1/4 cup olive oil
3 tablespoons granulated sugar
3 tablespoons lemon juice
1/2 teaspoon salt
1/4 teaspoon black pepper
3/4 cup water

1. Cut stems from okra.
2. In a skillet, cook okra over medium heat in olive oil for five minutes, stirring occasionally.
3. Add sugar, lemon juice, salt and pepper.
4. Toss lightly for one minute.
5. Add water.
6. Cover and simmer for 20 minutes, or until okra is tender.

Serves 4.

This is a soul food favorite that is customarily eaten on New Year's Day.

BLACK-EYED PEAS

2 quarts water
2-1/2 cups dried black-eyed peas
1/2 pound slab bacon or ham hocks
1 medium-sized onion (diced)
1/2 teaspoon salt
1/2 teaspoon black pepper
1/2 teaspoon crushed red peppers
1/2 garlic clove
1/4 teaspoon sugar

1. Wash the peas well.
2. Soak for at least three hours or overnight. Drain beans.
3. Place all ingredients in a cooking pot and cook for two and one-half to three hours, keeping just at a boil, adding more water if necessary. The final consistency should be rather soupy.

Serves 6 to 8.

Make these small and you can use them for appetizers.

POTATO CROQUETTES

2-1/4 cups cooked potatoes (riced)
1-1/2 tablespoons melted butter
1 teaspoon cream
1/2 teaspoon salt
1/8 teaspoon black pepper
1 egg yolk
1/4 teaspoon celery salt
1/4 teaspoon onion juice
1/2 cup cracker crumbs

1. Beat egg yolk.
2. Add melted butter, cream, salt, pepper, celery salt and onion juice. Stir to mix thoroughly.
3. Add potatoes and whip the mixture to combine.
4. Shape the croquettes by rolling one rounded tablespoon of the mixture into a ball and then flattening slightly to get the effect you want.
5. Roll in cracker crumbs.
6. Deep fry in fat or corn oil at 390° F. for at least one minute.
7. Remove from fat and drain.

Yields 18 to 20 croquettes.

Sue Heinz gave us this recipe which she calls ...

FAVORITE POTATOES

4 large potatoes (preferably Idaho potatoes)
1 stick butter
1 teaspoon seasoned salt
1/2 teaspoon black pepper
1/3 cup grated Parmesan cheese
2 tablespoons parsley flakes

1. Preheat oven to 325° F.
2. Peel, rinse and dry potatoes.
3. Cut lengthwise in slices about 1/4-inch thick and place overlapping in a large, buttered, baking dish.
4. Sprinkle with the salt and pepper.
5. Cut the butter into small pieces and dot over the top of the potatoes.
6. Sprinkle with the Parmesan cheese and garnish with the parsley flakes.
7. Cover with foil.
8. Bake at 325° F. for 1-1/2 hours or until potatoes are done.

Serves 4 to 6.

This is a delicious potato dish to serve with a roast.

SCALLOPED POTATOES

4 cups boiled potatoes, peeled and sliced thin
3-1/2 tablespoons butter
3-1/2 tablespoons regular flour
1-1/2 teaspoons salt
1/8 teaspoon black pepper
1-1/4 cup milk

1. Preheat oven to 400° F.
2. In a buttered baking dish make a layer of one-quarter of the potatoes.
3. Add one-quarter of the butter broken into bits.
4. Sprinkle with one-quarter of the flour, salt and pepper.
5. Repeat making layers until all ingredients are used.
6. Add the milk.
7. Bake at 400° F. for 1 hour.

Serves 5.

This is a good way to use those left-over potatoes.

POTATO SURPRISE

6 large, boiled potatoes (peeled)
2 fresh green peppers (sliced and seeded)
2 fresh tomatoes (sliced)
1 large onion (sliced)
1 cup shredded Cheddar cheese
1/2 teaspoon salt
1/8 teaspoon black pepper
3/4 cup milk

1. Preheat oven to 350° F.
2. In a buttered casserole, place the potatoes and sprinkle with half the salt and pepper.
3. Place the green peppers in a layer over the potatoes.
4. Add the tomatoes as a layer.
5. Cover with the onions and sprinkle with the remaining salt and pepper.
6. Cover with the cheese.
7. Pour in the milk.
8. Bake at 350° for 45 minutes.

Serves 8.

A real change from plain old potatoes.

SWEET POTATO CHIPS

3 large sweet potatoes (peeled, thinly sliced)
1-1/2 quarts cooking oil
powdered sugar to dredge

1. In a large pot, heat cooking oil over high heat (to 350° F. if you use a cooking thermometer)
2. Soak sweet potato slices in cold water for 10 minutes.
3. Drain slices on paper towels.
4. Drop slices in oil and fry until lightly browned.
5. Remove slices from oil with slotted spoon and drain on paper towels.
6. Sprinkle with powdered sugar.

Serves 6.

If you like stuffed Irish potatoes we are sure you will enjoy preparing sweet potatoes this way.

STUFFED SWEET POTATOES

6 medium-sized sweet potatoes
2 tablespoons melted butter or corn oil margarine
3 teaspoons cream
2 tablespoons brown sugar
1/2 teaspoon cinnamon

1. Wash sweet potatoes well and boil until tender.
2. Cut sweet potatoes in half lengthwise.
3. Scoop out most of the inside leaving enough to keep the casing firm.
4. To scooped-out sweet potato add butter, cream, sugar and cinnamon.
5. Refill the skins.
6. Place stuffed potatoes in shallow baking dish. Bake in preheated 425° F. oven for 5 minutes.

Serves 6.

A dinner at the Claudia Sanders Dinner House of Shelbyville wouldn't be complete without a taste of yams.

YAMS

8 cups finely chopped canned yams (drained and mashed)
1 cup white raisins
2 cups granulated sugar
1 pound butter (melted)
1/2 teaspoon mace
1/2 teaspoon cinnamon
1/2 cup fresh orange juice
1 pound miniature marshmallows
3 cups pineapple bits (optional)

1. In a cooking pot, cover raisins with water and cook until tender.
2. Drain in a colander.
3. Combine all other ingredients with the raisins and mix thoroughly.
4. Heat before serving.

Serves 6 to 8.

You might want to try your Thanksgiving yams this way.

PECAN YAMS

2 pounds yams (or sweet potatoes)
1 tablespoon grated orange rind
1 cup orange juice
2 tablespoons melted butter
1/3 cup brown sugar
1/2 cup honey
1/2 teaspoon mace
3/4 cup pecans (finely chopped)

1. Wash yams (or sweet potatoes).
2. Boil until tender, but slightly undercooked.
3. Peel, slice lengthwise and place in a greased baking dish. Set aside.
4. Mix all other ingredients thoroughly and pour over yams (or sweet potatoes).
5. Bake in preheated 300° oven for one hour.

Serves 8 to 10.

The chances are that your guests will ask for a second helping of Creamed Spinach. They do at the Claudia Sanders Dinner House of Shelbyville!

CREAMED SPINACH

1 10-ounce package of frozen chopped spinach
2 strips bacon (chopped fine)
1-1/2 tablespoons onion (chopped fine)
1 cup half-and-half
1-1/2 tablespoons butter
1 tablespoon flour
3/4 teaspoon salt
1/4 teaspoon black pepper

1. Thaw and cook spinach for 4 minutes in salted boiling water.
2. Drain and set aside.
3. In a skillet, brown the bacon and onion.
4. Add salt and pepper to bacon and onion. Set aside.
5. Bring the half-and-half to a boil in a cooking pot.
6. Melt the butter in a saucepan and add flour. Mix thoroughly and combine with the half-and-half. Cook until mixture thickens.
7. Add the spinach, bacon and onions to the half-and-half. Stir thoroughly and heat.

Serves 4.

A good company dish. If any members of your family do not like spinach, this just might make them change their minds.

SPINACH CASSEROLE

2 10-ounce packages frozen spinach, cooked and drained
1 5-ounce can water chestnuts, drained and thinly sliced
1 10-ounce package frozen Welsh rarebit (thawed)
8 slices bacon, crisp-cooked and crumbled
1/2 of 3-1/2-ounce can French fried onion rings

1. Preheat oven to 350° F.
2. Combine cooked spinach, water chestnuts and one-half of the Welsh rarebit in a 20x6x1-1/2-inch baking dish.
3. Top with bacon and spread remaining rarebit evenly over all.
4. Top with onion rings.
5. Bake uncovered at 350° F. for 15 minutes.

Serves 6.

A slightly different version of creamed spinach.

SPINACH SOUFFLÉ

1 pound frozen, chopped spinach
1/4 cup flour
1-1/2 cups half-and-half
1/2 cup bacon (fried crisp and chopped)
1/4 cup onion (chopped fine)
1/4 teaspoon garlic powder
3 tablespoons melted butter
1/2 teaspoon salt
1/2 teaspoon black pepper

1. Boil spinach until thoroughly cooked.
2. Drain and place in a large casserole.
3. Fry bacon and onion together.
4. Put in the casserole with the spinach.
5. Sprinkle with garlic powder and mix well. Set aside.
6. In a saucepan, combine the half-and-half, butter, flour, salt and pepper.
7. Stir well and cook over medium heat until thick.
8. Pour over the spinach and stir to mix.
9. Bake in preheated 350° F. oven until hot and bubbly.

Serves 6.

The Parmesan cheese in this recipe is optional and may be omitted
if you prefer.

BAKED YELLOW SQUASH

4 yellow squash
1 stick butter
2 tablespoons finely chopped onion
2 tablespoons parsley flakes
1 teaspoon salt
1/2 teaspoon black pepper
1/3 cup grated Parmesan cheese

1. Parboil whole, unpeeled squash for about 15 minutes.
2. Drain, cut stem end off and cut in half lengthwise.
3. Place in baking pan cut side up.
4. Sprinkle with the salt and pepper.
5. Cut butter into small pieces and sprinkle over top of squash.
6. Sprinkle with onion, parsley flakes and Parmesan cheese.
7. Bake in preheated 350° F. oven for one-half hour.

Serves 4.

The cheese makes this a delightful change from plain stewed tomatoes.

BAKED TOMATOES AND CHEESE

6 ripe tomatoes (scalded and peeled)
1-1/2 tablespoons melted butter
3 slices toasted white bread
1/4 cup yellow cheese (grated)
1 teaspoon salt
1/8 teaspoon black pepper

1. Preheat oven to 400° F.
2. In a small dish crumble toast and mix with the melted butter.
3. Cut the tomatoes into small pieces and put into a baking dish.
4. Season the tomatoes with the salt and pepper.
5. Cover the tomatoes with the toast.
6. Sprinkle the grated cheese over the top.
7. Bake at 400° F. for 30 minutes.

Serves 5.

These two vegetables make a real nice combination and will enhance your meal.

BAKED TOMATOES WITH LIMA BEANS

4 cups fresh lima beans
2 cups canned tomatoes
2 tablespoons butter
1 tablespoon finely chopped onion
1-1/4 teaspoons salt
1 cup water

1. Preheat oven to 375° F.
2. Run tomatoes through a food grinder or strainer.
3. Combine with lima beans. Set aside.
4. Melt the butter and add the salt and onion.
5. Combine with tomatoes and lima beans.
6. Add the water and mix the ingredients well.
7. Pour into buttered baking dish and cover.
8. Bake at 375° F. for 1 hour.

Serves 6.

Breaded tomatoes go well with any meal and the way people eat them you will have to admit they go very fast!

BREADED TOMATOES

4 cups canned tomatoes (if whole, squeeze or mash them)
1/2 cup vegetable oil
1 teaspoon salt
1/4 teaspoon black pepper
1/2 cup granulated sugar
1/2 cup chopped onion
1/2 teaspoon Durkee Charcoal Seasoning
2 tablespoons butter
2 tablespoons flour
3 slices white bread (toasted brown and cut into small squares)

1. Combine tomatoes, vegetable oil, onion, salt, pepper, and charcoal seasoning.
2. Cook over medium heat until mixture boils.
3. While tomatoes are cooking, melt butter and add flour, mixing thoroughly.
4. Add this to the tomato mixture.
5. Cook until mixture thickens. Stir to keep from sticking.
6. Add the sugar and simmer for 2 or 3 minutes.
7. Mix in the toasted bread pieces just before serving.

Serves 6.

This makes an excellent side dish and goes well with almost any other vegetable.

DEVILED TOMATOES

4 medium-sized tomatoes
6 tablespoons butter or corn oil margarine
2 hard-cooked eggs (use yolks only)
1 egg, beaten
1 teaspoon powdered sugar
1 teaspoon prepared mustard
2 tablespoons vinegar
1/4 teaspoon salt
1/8 teaspoon black pepper

1. Peel and slice the tomatoes.
2. Put 2 tablespoons of the butter in a skillet and fry the tomatoes lightly, turning often.
3. Melt the rest of the butter in the top of a double boiler.
4. Remove from heat.
5. Mash the two hard-cooked egg yolks and add to the melted butter.
6. Add the powdered sugar, mustard, vinegar, salt and black pepper to the butter.
7. Add the beaten egg, stirring the mixture well.
8. Cook until mixture thickens. Stir constantly.
9. Put tomatoes in a serving dish and pour mixture over them.

Serves 6.

This makes an attractive garnish for a meat dish. We like them served as a vegetable with our meal.

FRIED GREEN TOMATOES

6 green tomatoes
1 egg, well beaten
1 cup cracker crumbs
2 tablespoons melted butter
1/2 teaspoon salt
1/8 teaspoon black pepper

1. Wash and slice tomatoes. Set aside.
2. Combine the butter, salt and pepper.
3. Brush butter over the tomatoes.
4. Dip the tomatoes in the cracker crumbs, then in the egg, and again in the cracker crumbs.
5. Fry in buttered skillet for 7 or 8 minutes. Turn often.

Serves 6.

These grilled tomatoes can take the place of a salad if you want to have a quick meal without a lot of bother.

GRILLED TOMATOES

4 ripe, medium-sized tomatoes
3/4 cup Italian dressing
4 teaspoons bread crumbs (crushed fine and buttered with melted butter)
1 teaspoon salt
1/2 teaspoon black pepper
1/4 cup grated Parmesan cheese

1. Preheat oven to 350° F.
2. Wash tomatoes and cut a slice from the stem end.
3. Place in a baking pan cut end up.
4. Brush liberally with Italian dressing (see Italian Dressing, page 54, if you want to make your own)
5. Sprinkle tops of tomatoes with buttered bread crumbs.
6. Season with the salt and pepper.
7. Sprinkle with the Parmesan cheese.
8. Bake at 350° F. for one half hour, or until tomatoes are done.

Serves 4.

This is a real husband (or boyfriend) pleaser.

ZUCCHINI-TOMATO CASSEROLE

1/4 cup olive oil
1 large onion, peeled and thinly sliced.
6 very small zucchini (cut in 1/2-inch slices)
2 quarts canned tomatoes (we like to use our own home-canned)
1 teaspoon salt
1/2 teaspoon black pepper
2 teaspoons oregano
1/2 teaspoon monosodium glutamate

1. In a large iron skillet over medium-high heat, heat the olive oil.
2. Cook onion in olive oil until transparent.
3. Add zucchini to onion and continue cooking until tender. Stir occasionally.
4. Add salt, pepper, oregano and monosodium glutamate.
5. Add tomatoes.
6. When mixture comes to a boil, turn down to simmer, and simmer for 30 minutes.

Serves 8.

DESSERTS
SAUCES
CONFECTIONS
CAKES AND PIES

Christine Montgomery's Bread Pudding is a real palate pleaser.

BREAD PUDDING

8 cold biscuits
2 cups milk
1 cup granulated sugar
2 tablespoons melted butter, or margarine
1 teaspoon cinnamon

1. Preheat oven to 350° F.
2. Crumble biscuits in a large baking dish. Set aside.
3. Combine milk, melted butter, sugar and cinnamon.
4. Pour milk mixture over crumbled biscuits. Stir well.
5. Bake at 350° F. for 30 minutes.
6. Remove from oven and cover with Bread Pudding Sauce.

Serves 8.

BREAD PUDDING SAUCE

2 tablespoons instant flour
1 cup water
1/2 cup sugar
1/4 teaspoon cinnamon or lemon juice

1. Combine all ingredients and mix thoroughly.
2. Cook over medium heat until sauce thickens.
3. Serve either hot or cold.

We think you will enjoy this pudding either hot or cold.

RICE PUDDING

1 cup cooked rice
2 cups milk
2 eggs (yolks and whites separated)
1/2 cup sugar
1/4 teaspoon salt
1/4 teaspoon cinnamon
1/2 teaspoon vanilla

1. Scald the milk and add the rice. Set aside.
2. Beat the egg yolks and add the sugar.
3. Slowly combine with the milk mixture and season with the salt and cinnamon.
4. Cook in double boiler until the mixture thickens.
5. Fold in egg whites beaten stiff and add the vanilla.

Serves 6.

Kids will love these. Have some on the table when they come home from school.

FRUIT FRITTERS

1 cup sifted flour
1-1/2 teaspoons baking powder
1 teaspoon salt
1/2 teaspoon cinnamon (nutmeg, mace, or ginger)
1/3 cup brown sugar
1 egg, beaten
2/3 cup milk
1 tablespoon vegetable oil

1. Sift flour, baking powder, salt, cinnamon (or other spice) and sugar together. Set aside.
2. Combine egg, milk and vegetable oil.
3. Blend flour mixture into egg mixture until smooth.
4. Coat your choice of fruit with this batter.
5. Deep fry at 375° F. in cooking oil until golden brown. (About 1-1/2 minutes).
6. Drain. Sprinkle with confectioners' sugar if you desire.

The following fruits may be used:
    Pineapple slices, or spears.
    Bananas, halved or quartered.
    Canned cling peach halves.
    Apple slices, or wedges.

This batter may also be used to coat slices of fish or other seafood, or vegetables. In this case, omit the brown sugar from the recipe.

Yield varies according to how much fruit you use.

Canned peaches may be used in this cobbler but we prefer fresh peaches in ours.

MARGE STUCKER'S PEACH COBBLER

Cobbler:
    10 peaches
    4 tablespoons granulated sugar
    2 teaspoons cinnamon

Topping:
    1/2 cup butter
    1 cup granulated sugar
    2 eggs, well beaten

1. Preheat oven to 400° F.
2. Peel and halve peaches; remove seeds.
3. Line 13-1/2 x 8-3/4 x 1-3/4 inch baking dish with Cherry Settle's Pie Crust (unbaked)—see page 167.
4. Line unbaked pie crust with peach halves pit side up.
5. Sprinkle with granulated sugar and cinnamon.
6. Bake at 400° F. for 20 or 30 minutes, or until peaches are soft or crust is slightly browned.
7. While cobbler is cooking make topping by creaming butter, sugar and eggs together.
8. After cobbler has baked for 20 or 30 minutes cover with topping and continue baking at 400° F. for another 15 minutes.

Serves 12.

This is an especially good sauce to use over bread pudding, cobbler, or plain cake.

BUTTER-VANILLA SAUCE

1 pint cream
2 cups granulated sugar
2 cups light corn syrup
3 tablespoons butter
1 teaspoon vanilla
3/4 cup crushed pecans

1. Cream butter and sugar together.
2. Combine with cream and corn syrup.
3. Cook over medium heat until mixture reaches a rolling boil.
4. Remove from heat and add vanilla and nuts. Mix thoroughly.

Makes two pints sauce.

This chocolate sauce has many uses. We find it goes well with ice cream or bread pudding.

CHOCOLATE SAUCE

1 pint cream
1/3 cup granulated sugar
1/2 cup cocoa
1/2 cup sifted, all-purpose flour
1 teaspoon vanilla

1. Sift flour, sugar, and cocoa together.
2. Add cream and mix well.
3. Cook over medium heat until mixture thickens.
4. Remove from fire. Add vanilla and beat well.

Makes one pint sauce.

These can be used to line Charlotte Russe bowls or in any suitable fruit dessert, as well as just enjoyed by themselves.

LADY FINGERS

1/3 cup sifted cake flour
1/2 cup powdered sugar
3 egg whites
2 egg yolks
1/2 teaspoon salt
1 teaspoon vanilla

1. Preheat oven to 350° F.
2. Beat egg whites until stiff and moist.
3. Add sugar gradually and continue beating until thoroughly combined. Set aside.
4. In separate dish beat egg yolks until thick.
5. Add vanilla to egg yolks.
6. Combine egg yolks and egg whites.
7. Sift flour and salt together and fold in egg mixture. Be sure to combine thoroughly.
8. Bake at 350° F. for 12 to 15 minutes in lightly buttered Lady Finger tins, or on ungreased paper after shaping into 1x4-inch "fingers".

Yields 18 Lady Fingers.

Many kinds of desserts can be made with meringue shells. Fill them with crushed fruit, chocolate sauce, or ice cream.

MERINGUE SHELLS

4 egg whites (best at room temperature)
1-1/2 cups confectioners' sugar
1/4 teaspoon cream of tartar
1/4 teaspoon salt
1/4 teaspoon vanilla

1. Preheat oven to 250° F.
2. Add salt and cream of tartar to egg whites and beat until stiff.
3. Add one cup of the sugar and continue to beat until the mixture holds its shape.
4. Add the vanilla.
5. Fold in the remaining 1/2 cup sugar.
6. Cover a cookie sheet with wax paper and place the meringue mixture in mounds on this. Remove center part, or depress with a spoon, so meringues are cuplike.
7. Bake at 250° F. for 55 or 60 minutes.

Makes 6 meringues.

This is our family's favorite and we hope it will be yours, too.

ALMOND COOKIES

5 tablespoons granulated sugar
1 cup butter
2 cups sifted flour
1 pinch salt
1 cup almonds (ground)
1 teaspoon vanilla

1. Preheat oven to 275° F.
2. Cream butter and sugar.
3. Add other ingredients, mixing thoroughly.
4. Refrigerate to stiffen.
5. When firm, shape into crescents.
6. Bake on ungreased cookie sheet at 275° F. for 15 minutes.

(Other nuts, or even cheese, may be substituted.)
Yields 3 to 4 dozen cookies.

Good anytime, these will add festivity to your holidays.

KENTUCKY WALNUT BOURBON BALLS

1 cup powdered sugar
2-1/2 cups finely crushed vanilla wafers
2 tablespoons cocoa
1 cup walnuts (finely chopped)
3 tablespoons white corn syrup
1/4 cup Kentucky bourbon
1/2 teaspoon vanilla

1. Mix powdered sugar, vanilla wafers, cocoa and walnuts.
2. Add bourbon, corn syrup and vanilla.
3. Work into one-inch balls.
4. Roll balls in powdered sugar until completely covered.

Yields one to two dozen, depending on size you prefer.

This is an easy cake to make and has a satisfying flavor. We are sure your family will like it.

BLACK JAM CAKE

4 whole eggs
1 cup granulated sugar
1/2 cup Karo dark syrup
1 cup melted margarine
1 cup buttermilk
1 cup blackberry jam
1 cup raisins
1 teaspoon soda
1 tablespoon nutmeg
2 tablespoons cinnamon
1 teaspoon ground cloves
3 cups self-rising flour (sifted)
1 cup chopped fresh apples (peeled, cored and seeded)
2 tablespoons cocoa

1. Preheat oven to 350° F.
2. Sift together the flour, nutmeg, cinnamon, cloves and cocoa. Set aside.
3. Add soda to buttermilk.
4. Combine eggs, sugar, margarine and mix with the buttermilk and soda.
5. Add raisins, syrup, jam and apples to this mixture and then combine it with the flour mixture.
6. Pour into two 9-inch square baking pans.
7. Bake at 350° F. for 30 minutes.
8. Remove from oven and cool.
9. Cover with icing (see page 147).

Makes one 2-layer, 9-inch square cake.

ICING FOR BLACK JAM CAKE

4 cups brown sugar
1 cup evaporated milk
1 cup butter
2 teaspoons vanilla
1/4 teaspoon salt

1. Combine all ingredients, working the butter in well.
2. Bring to a boil and boil for one minute.
3. Remove from heat and beat for one minute or until the mixture will spread.
4. Use as directed.

Yields enough icing for one Black Jam Cake including between the layers.

Jeanette Murphy advises you to have the ingredients at room temperature when you bake her Cherry Nut Cake.

CHERRY NUT CAKE

2-1/2 cups sifted cake flour
1 cup milk
1-1/4 cups granulated sugar
1/2 cup butter or shortening
2 whole eggs
1/2 cup maraschino cherries (chopped; save juice for the frosting)
1/2 cup chopped pecans
3 teaspoons baking powder
1/4 teaspoon salt
1 teaspoon vanilla

1. Preheat oven to 325° F.
2. Sift flour, salt and baking powder together. Set aside.
3. Soften butter, or shortening, with mixer at medium speed.
4. Add sugar gradually, beating until mixture is smooth.
5. Add eggs to sugar and butter and beat for 1 or 2 minutes.
6. Add flour mixture and milk to egg mixture alternately, using about half of each at a time. Beat for 2 or 3 minutes, or until smooth.
7. Stir in vanilla.
8. Dredge the cherries and nuts with flour and then fold into cake batter.
9. Pour into two well-greased and floured 9-inch cake pans.
10. Bake at 325° F. for 30 minutes, or until tests show cake is done. (If baked in a gas stove, place a small pan of water in the bottom of the oven).
11. Cool on a cake rack.
12. Cover sides and tops with Jeanette Murphy's Seven Minute Frosting.

Yields one 2-layer, 9-inch cake.

SEVEN MINUTE FROSTING

1-1/2 cups granulated sugar
2 egg whites, unbeaten
1/4 teaspoon cream of tartar
1/8 teaspoon salt
1 teaspoon vanilla
1 tablespoon light corn syrup
juice saved from cherries plus enough water to make ½ cup.

1. Mix all ingredients together in top of double boiler.
2. Place over boiling water.
3. Mix with mixer at low speed to break down egg whites for about 2 minutes.
4. Increase speed to high and beat for seven minutes, or until stiff enough to stand up in peaks.
5. Use as directed for Cherry Nut Cake.

For you gardeners: remember all that zucchini? Well, here's what you can do with some of it.

CHOCOLATE ZUCCHINI CAKE

2-1/2 cups flour
1/2 cup cocoa
1 teaspoon cinnamon
2-1/2 teaspoons baking powder
1-1/2 teaspoons baking soda
3/4 cup butter
2 cups granulated sugar
3 eggs
2 teaspoons vanilla
2 cups shredded *raw* zucchini
1/4 cup milk
1 cup chopped pecans
1 cup confectioners' sugar
1 tablespoon orange juice

1.   Preheat oven to 350° F.
2.   Sift together flour, cocoa, cinnamon, baking powder and soda. Set aside.
3.   In mixing bowl, cream butter and sugar until light and fluffy.
4.   Add eggs and beat well.
5.   Add vanilla and zucchini and blend thoroughly.
6.   Blend in flour mixture alternately with milk.
7.   Fold in pecans.
8.   Bake at 350° F. in greased bundt pan for 50 minutes.
9.   Cool in pan before removing.
10. Make a glaze of 1 cup confectioners' sugar and 1 tablespoon orange juice heated in saucepan until clear.
11. Drizzle glaze over cooled cake.

Makes one 10-inch cake.

You may prefer to use your own favorite frosting on this cake.

DEVIL'S FOOD CAKE

2 cups sifted cake flour
1 cup brown sugar
1/4 cup granulated sugar
1/2 cup cocoa
1/2 cup butter
2 eggs, well beaten
2 teaspoons baking powder
1 teaspoon cinnamon
1/2 teaspoon salt
1 teaspoon vanilla
1 cup milk

1. Preheat oven to 350° F.
2. Sift flour, cocoa, cinnamon, salt and baking powder together. Set aside.
3. Combine the butter, sugars and eggs. Beat well.
4. Add the vanilla to egg mixture.
5. Add flour and milk alternately in small amounts to the egg mixture. Beat after each addition until mixture is smooth.
6. Pour into 2 well-greased 9-inch cake pans.
7. Bake at 350° F. for 25 to 30 minutes.
8. Cover tops and sides with frosting (see page 152).

Yields one 2-layer, 9-inch cake.

FROSTING FOR DEVIL'S FOOD CAKE

2 cups brown sugar
1 cup granulated sugar
1-1/2 cups milk
2-1/2 tablespoons butter
1/4 teaspoon cinnamon
1 teaspoon vanilla

1. Bring milk to boil and add the sugars. Stir while cooking.
2. Add butter.
3. Remove from fire and cool to lukewarm.
4. Add vanilla and cinnamon.
5. Beat until creamy.
6. Spread over tops and sides of cake.

Yields enough frosting for one 2-layer, 9-inch cake.

The Christmastime favorite.

FRUIT CAKE I

3 cups sifted flour
1 cup butter
1-1/2 teaspoons baking powder
1-1/2 cups pecan pieces
1/2 cup chopped candied pineapple
1 cup raisins
1 cup currants
1/2 cup candied cherries
1/2 cup chopped citron
1/2 cup chopped lemon peel
1/2 cup chopped orange peel
6 eggs well-beaten
2-1/4 cups powdered sugar
1 teaspoon nutmeg
1/2 teaspoon cinnamon
1/2 teaspoon cloves
1 teaspoon allspice
1/2 cup fresh orange juice

1. Preheat oven to 300° F.
2. Sift flour and baking powder together. Set aside.
3. Cream the butter.
4. Add the sugar to the butter.
5. Combine butter and the eggs.
6. Add the flour to the butter and eggs, mixing thoroughly.
7. Add the orange juice. (You may substitute 1/2 cup milk or 1/2 cup whiskey.)
8. Put in the fruits and nuts and season with the spices, blending all thoroughly.
9. Bake at 300° F. for 2 to 2-1/2 hours in a well-greased and floured 10-inch tube pan.

Makes 1 10-inch fruit cake.

This is Gladys Biggers' recipe for the fruit cake she makes each Christmas season.

FRUIT CAKE II

9 cups flour (sifted)
2 cups butter
2 cups dark molasses
2 cups brown sugar
1 cup blackberry jam
2 tablespoons allspice
2 tablespoons cinnamon
2 tablespoons nutmeg
2 tablespoons ground cloves
2 cups buttermilk
2 teaspoons baking soda
6 whole eggs (or 12 yolks, if you prefer)
1-1/2 pounds chopped English walnuts
2 pounds raisins
2 pounds pitted dates
1/2 cup strong, boiled coffee
1 cup candied cherries
1 cup candied pineapple

1. Preheat oven to 275° F.
2. Mix sugar and butter thoroughly.
3. Add the coffee, molasses, eggs and jam and beat thoroughly.
4. Mix buttermilk and soda and set aside.
5. Sift 6 cups of the flour with the allspice, cinnamon, nutmeg and cloves and combine this with the buttermilk and soda.
6. Add sugar, coffee and egg mixture to this.
7. Put in the raisins, dates, walnuts, cherries and pineapple, combining thoroughly.
8. Sift in the remaining three cups flour to make a thick batter.
9. Pour into a greased and floured 10-inch tube pan. With batter left over, you can make small cakes.
10. Bake at 275°F. for 2-1/2 hours.

Makes one 10-inch cake, plus several smaller ones.

For variety, try this with peaches or apricots.

PINEAPPLE UPSIDE-DOWN CAKE

1-1/2 cups sifted flour
1/2 cup milk
5 tablespoons butter or margarine
3/4 cup granulated sugar
3/4 cup brown sugar
1 egg, beaten
1-1/2 teaspoons baking powder
1/4 teaspoon salt
1/2 teaspoon vanilla
1 small can sliced pineapple

1. Preheat oven to 375° F.
2. Sift flour, baking powder and salt together. Set aside.
3. In separate dish cream 3 tablespoons of the butter and add the granulated sugar.
4. Add egg to butter mixture.
5. Add flour and milk to egg mixture, alternating a small amount at a time and beating each time until mixture is smooth.
6. Add vanilla.
7. Melt remaining 2 tablespoons butter into a 9-inch pie pan.
8. Add brown sugar and stir until well mixed with the butter.
9. Place pineapple slices in brown sugar mixture.
10. Cover with cake batter.
11. Bake at 375° F. for 25 minutes, or until done.
12. Cool and remove carefully from pie pan so that fruit is on top.

Yields one 9-inch, 1-layer cake.

Use your favorite frosting on this easy-to-prepare plain cake.

PLAIN CAKE

2 cups sifted cake flour
1 cup granulated sugar
2 eggs, beaten
3/4 cup milk
3 teaspoons baking powder
1/4 teaspoon salt
1 teaspoon vanilla
1/4 teaspoon almond extract
6 tablespoons butter or corn oil margarine

1. Preheat oven to 375° F.
2. Sift flour, baking powder and salt together. Set aside.
3. Cream the butter and gradually add the sugar.
4. Add eggs to butter.
5. Add vanilla and almond extract to eggs and butter.
6. Add flour and milk alternately, small amounts at a time. Beat the batter to mix the ingredients thoroughly.
7. Pour into two 8-inch, well-greased cake pans.
8. Bake at 375° F. for 30 to 35 minutes.

Yields one 8-inch 2-layer cake.

Don't throw away those cold potatoes! Make this cake with them.

MASHED IRISH POTATO CAKE

1 cup mashed cold potatoes
2 cups sifted flour
1/2 cup sweet milk
4 eggs
2 cups granulated sugar
1 cup butter
3/4 cup cocoa
2 teaspoons baking powder
1 teaspoon cloves
1 teaspoon cinnamon
1 teaspoon nutmeg
1 cup walnut meats (halved)

1. Preheat oven to 375° F.
2. Sift together the flour, sugar, cocoa, baking powder, cloves, cinnamon and nutmeg.
3. Work in the butter.
4. Mix eggs in the flour mixture and beat with spoon until mixture is creamy.
5. Add milk gradually and beat well.
6. Add walnuts.
7. Add the potatoes and mix thoroughly.
8. Pour into two greased 9-inch cake pans.
9. Bake at 375° F. for one hour.
10. Cool and cover with your favorite icing.

Yields one 2-layer, 9-inch cake.

This is another of Gladys Biggers' excellent cake recipes.

PRUNE CAKE

   2 cups sifted self-rising flour
   1/2 cup granulated sugar
   1 cup buttermilk
   1 cup chopped prunes
   2-1/2 teaspoons mixed spices
   1 cup corn oil
   1 cup chopped pecans
   1 teaspoon baking soda
   1/2 teaspoon salt
   3 whole eggs

1. Preheat oven to 350° F.
2. Mix together the flour, sugar, salt and corn oil. Be sure to mix thoroughly.
3. Add eggs and spices and beat thoroughly.
4. Add prunes and pecans and mix well.
5. Combine the soda and buttermilk and add to flour mixture.
6. Pour into a 10x10x2-inch, greased and floured pan.
7. Bake at 350° F. for 40 to 45 minutes.
8. Cool and cover with sauce (see below).

Makes one 10x10-inch cake.

SAUCE FOR PRUNE CAKE

   1/2 cup buttermilk
   1 cup granulated sugar
   2 teaspoons vanilla
   1/2 teaspoon baking soda

1. Mix all ingredients thoroughly.
2. Cook two minutes over medium heat.
3. Use as directed.

This version of an old recipe won a Blue-ribbon at the Shelby County (Ky.) Fair in 1976 for its creator, Marge Stucker.

DARK RUM CAKE

1 18-1/2-oz. package yellow cake mix
4-ounce package vanilla pudding
1 cup corn oil
1/2 cup water
1/2 cup dark rum
4 eggs, beaten
1/2 to 3/4 cup pecans or other nuts (chopped)

1. Preheat oven to 350° F.
2. Blend cake mix, vanilla pudding, corn oil, water, rum and eggs in a large mixing bowl. Set aside.
3. Sprinkle nuts in bottom of well greased and floured 12-inch bundt pan.
4. Pour batter on nuts.
5. Bake at 350° F. for exactly 55 minutes.
6. Let cool in pan for 5 minutes.
7. Drizzle topping on cake while still in pan, in small amounts every 15 minutes until topping is used up.
8. When cake is cool, turn out on wax paper on a plate. (This is a very moist cake and the wax paper will prevent sticking.)

TOPPING

1/2 cup granulated sugar
1/4 cup dark rum
1/4 cup water
1 stick corn oil margarine

1. Mix all ingredients thoroughly.
2. Cook over medium heat for 5 minutes and cool slightly.

Yields one 12-inch cake.

We find this to be one of the few good ways to use frozen strawberries.

STRAWBERRY CAKE

1 cup frozen sliced strawberries
1 18-1/2-oz. box white cake mix
1 box strawberry-flavored gelatin (3-oz size)
2 teaspoons all-purpose flour
3/4 cup vegetable oil
1/2 cup cold water
3 eggs

1. Preheat oven to 350° F.
2. Mix cake mix, gelatin and flour.
3. Add oil, eggs and water.
4. Beat 2 or 3 minutes with electric mixer at high speed.
5. Add strawberries.
6. Beat again for 3 minutes or until thoroughly mixed.
7. Pour into 3 8-inch, greased cake pans.
8. Bake at 350° F. for 30 to 35 minutes.
9. Cool cakes on rack before frosting.

FROSTING

1 box confectioners' sugar
1 stick margarine
1 cup sliced frozen strawberries

1. Cream sugar and margarine together.
2. Gradually add strawberries while beating at low speed with electric beater until completely mixed.
3. Frost cake between layers and on the top and sides.
4. Cool in refrigerator until ready to serve.

Yields one 8-inch, 3-layer cake.

This cake has no frosting and makes a good coffee cake.

SOUR CREAM CAKE

3 cups sifted flour
3 cups granulated sugar
1 cup sour cream
1 cup butter, or margarine
6 eggs, separated
1/4 teaspoon baking soda
1/2 teaspoon vanilla
1/2 teaspoon mace

1. Preheat oven to 300° F.
2. Cream butter (or margarine) until fluffy.
3. Add egg yolks one at a time.
4. In a separate dish add soda to sour cream.
5. Alternate flour with sour cream mixture, butter (or margarine) and sugar.
6. In another dish beat egg whites until stiff but not dry.
7. Fold in egg whites to flour, sour cream, butter (or margarine) and sugar mixture; mix gently, but thoroughly.
8. Add vanilla and mace.
9. Bake at 300° F. for 1-1/2 hours in greased 8x8x2-inch cake pan.

Yields one 8x8x2-inch cake.

Best at breakfast, this Coffee Cake also makes a good midday snack.

WALNUT COFFEE CAKE

1-1/2 cups sifted flour
2 eggs, well beaten
1/2 cup sugar
1 teaspoon pure orange juice
2 teaspoons baking powder
1/2 teaspoon salt
1 cup milk
3 tablespoons melted butter
1/2 cup black walnuts (chopped)
1/2 teaspoon cinnamon, or enough to sprinkle over top
1/2 stick butter

1. Preheat oven to 400° F.
2. Sift flour, baking powder, salt and sugar together. Set aside.
3. In separate bowl mix milk, eggs, orange juice and melted butter.
4. Combine flour and milk mixtures.
5. Add walnuts and beat mixture until smooth.
6. Pour into buttered 8x8x2-inch pan.
7. Break 1/2 stick butter into small pieces and speckle on top of batter.
8. Dust with cinnamon.
9. Bake at 400° F. for 25 minutes.

Yields one 8x8x2-inch cake.

A delicious change from apple pie.

APPLE SLICES

    4 cups sifted flour
    1-1/2 cups shortening
    3/4 cup granulated sugar
    10 or 12 apples (peeled, cored and sliced)
    2 eggs, separated
    1 cup milk
    1/4 cup brown sugar
    1/2 teaspoon salt
    1/2 teaspoon baking powder
    1 teaspoon cinnamon
    1 teaspoon nutmeg
    1 tablespoon lemon juice
    powdered sugar to garnish

1.   Preheat oven to 400° F.
2.   Beat egg yolks with milk. Set aside.
3.   Mix flour, salt, baking powder and shortening. Cut like pie crust.
4.   Add egg mix to flour mix.
5.   Put one-half of this mixture into 10x6x1-1/2-inch baking pan.
6.   Mix peeled and sliced apples with white and brown sugar, cinnamon, nutmeg and lemon juice.
7.   Place apple mixture on dough in baking pan.
8.   Roll rest of flour mixture between two pieces of wax paper, remove and place on top of apples in baking pan.
9.   Beat the 2 egg whites until stiff and spread on top of crust.
10. Bake at 400° F. for 10 minutes.
11. Lower temperature to 350° and bake for 35 minutes.
12. Remove from oven and sprinkle with powdered sugar to garnish.

Serves 8.

Pecans as well as walnuts may be used in this pie.

BROWNIE PIE

3 egg whites
3/4 cup granulated sugar
3/4 cup fine chocolate wafer crumbs
1/2 cup chopped black walnuts
1/2 teaspoon vanilla
dash salt

1. Preheat oven to 325° F.
2. Beat egg whites until very stiff.
3. Add sugar slowly.
4. Fold in wafer crumbs, nuts, salt and vanilla.
5. Bake at 325° F. for 40 minutes in a 9-inch pie pan.
6. Cool.
7. Top with sweetened whipped cream or vanilla ice cream.

Serves 8.

Chess Pie is as much a favorite on the family table as it is at the Claudia Sanders Dinner House of Shelbyville.

CHESS PIE

2 cups sugar
1/2 cup butter
1 tablespoon all-purpose flour
5 well-beaten egg yolks
1 cup half-and-half
1 teaspoon vanilla
1 tablespoon lemon juice
1/2 teaspoon cinnamon
1/2 teaspoon nutmeg

1. Preheat oven to 350° F.
2. Cream butter and sugar together.
3. Add egg yolks, half-and-half, vanilla, lemon juice, flour, cinnamon and nutmeg.
4. Beat thoroughly.
5. Pour into 9-inch pie crust. (See Cherry Settle's Pie Crust—page 167).
6. Bake at 350° F. for one hour.

Makes one 9-inch pie.

This promises to be one of the best pies you have ever made.

CHOCOLATE CHESS PIE

1/2 cup shredded coconut
3/4 cup pecan halves
5 tablespoons powdered cocoa
1-1/2 cups sugar
1/4 cup butter
2 eggs, beaten
1/2 cup evaporated milk

1. Preheat oven to 400° F.
2. Mix all ingredients thoroughly.
3. Pour into 9-inch unbaked pie shell.
4. Bake at 400° F. for 30 minutes.
5. Cool.

We find this best served with a scoop of vanilla ice cream.

Serves 8.

The butter adds a special flavor and flaky texture to this crust. This was a Blue-Ribbon winner at the Shelby County (Ky.) Fair (1979).

CHERRY SETTLE'S PIE CRUST

2 cups sifted all-purpose flour
1 teaspoon salt
1/3 cup shortening
1/3 cup butter
5 to 6 tablespoons ice water

1. Sift flour and salt together in large mixing bowl.
2. Cut shortening and butter into the flour with a heavy fork or pastry blender until it forms particles about the size of a pea.
3. Add ice water a few drops at a time and toss. The dough should be just moist enough to hold together in a ball, but not wet.
4. Refrigerate dough wrapped in wax paper for 30 minutes before rolling it out.
5. Cut dough in half.
6. Roll out on floured board.
7. Place in greased 9-inch pie pans.
8. Baking temperature will depend on type of pies you are making.

Yields two 9-inch pie crusts.

Your family will love you when you serve this pie.

CHERRY PIE

1 nine-inch unbaked pie shell (see Cherry Settle's Pie Crust—page 167).
2 cans tart cherries, pitted. (Drain and reserve the juice.) (16-oz size)
1-1/4 cups granulated sugar
1/2 cup sifted flour
1/2 teaspoon salt
3/4 cup juice from the cherries
2 tablespoons butter
7 drops pure almond extract
15 drops red food coloring

1. Preheat oven to 400° F.
2. Sift together the flour, sugar and salt.
3. Stir in the cherry juice.
4. Place on stove over medium heat and cook until mixture thickens.
5. Cook for another minute.
6. Add butter, almond extract, cherries and food coloring.
7. Pour into pie shell and top with strips of pastry (see Cherry Settle's Pie Crust—page 167), lattice fashion.
8. Bake at 400° F. for 30 minutes, or until crust is golden brown.

Yields one 9-inch pie.

Chocolate Chip Pie is a real favorite at the Claudia Sanders Dinner House.

CHOCOLATE CHIP PIE

1 cup granulated sugar
1/2 cup flour
2 eggs
1/4 pound butter, melted and cooled slightly
1 cup broken pecans (you may substitute almonds or walnuts)
1 6-oz. package semi-sweet chocolate chips
1 teaspoon vanilla

1. Preheat oven to 325° F.
2. Beat eggs slightly.
3. Add sugar and stir thoroughly.
4. Add the flour, stirring in well.
5. Add the butter.
6. Add chips and pecan pieces.
7. Add vanilla.
8. Pour into frozen 9-inch pie crust. (Or see Cherry Settle's Pie Crust—page 167).
9. Bake at 325° F. for one hour.

Serves eight.

This pie is best when served warm, especially so right after being baked. We find it delicious when served with whipped cream or a small amount of ice cream. That's the way we serve it at the Claudia Sanders Dinner House and the guests love it.

When Christine Montgomery wants to please her guests she serves them her Coconut Pie.

CHRISTINE'S COCONUT PIE

1 9-inch prebaked pie crust (see Cherry Settle's Pie Crust—page 167)
1/4 cup shredded coconut
1 13-ounce can unsweetened condensed milk
1/4 cup water
2-1/2 tablespoons sifted flour
3/4 cup granulated sugar
2 tablespoons margarine
6 egg yolks, beaten (save the whites for the meringue)
1 teaspoon vanilla

1. Preheat oven to 400° F.
2. Mix milk, water, egg yolks, margarine and vanilla. Set aside.
3. Mix flour, sugar and coconut.
4. Combine the two mixtures, blending thoroughly.
5. Cook in double boiler until mixture thickens.
6. Put in prebaked pie crust and top with meringue.
7. Bake at 400° F. just long enough to brown the meringue.

MERINGUE

6 egg whites
2 tablespoons powdered sugar

1. Beat egg whites until stiff, but moist.
2. Add powdered sugar and beat for at least another minute.
3. Use as directed for Christine's Coconut Pie.

Yields one 9-inch pie.

Tired of cooking and want a good dessert? Here's a pie you can make without lighting the oven.

FREEZER GRASSHOPPER PIE

 1 egg white
 2 tablespoons sugar
 1/3 cup light corn syrup
 1/2 pint heavy cream
 2 tablespoons white crème de cacao
 2 tablespoons green crème de menthe
 1 8-inch chocolate crust (chilled)
 dash of salt

1. Add dash of salt to egg white and beat until soft peaks form.
2. Beat sugar in gradually until mixture becomes smooth and glossy.
3. Add corn syrup a little at a time. Continue to beat until the mixture holds stiff, firm, straight peaks. Set aside.
4. Whip the heavy cream until stiff.
5. Fold the crème de cacao and crème de menthe into the whipped cream.
6. Fold whipped cream mixture into the egg white mixture.
7. Turn into the chocolate crust.
8. Freeze for 12 hours, or overnight.

Makes 1 8-inch pie.

CHOCOLATE CRUST FOR FREEZER GRASSHOPPER PIE

 1-1/3 cups chocolate wafer crumbs
 1/3 cup margarine

1. Mix the two ingredients well.
2. Press firmly on bottom and sides of the 8-inch pie pan.
3. Chill until set and ready to fill.

If the crust of the finished pie is hard to cut, dip bottom of pan in hot water for a second or two. The filling itself will not freeze hard.

This yummy, crumbly pie is another of Marge Stucker's creations. Try it with a ball of sharp Cheddar cheese on each slice.

PEAR-APPLE CRUMB PIE

3 cups sliced canned pears
2 cups sliced tart apples
1/3 cup granulated sugar
2 tablespoons flour
1/2 teaspoon cinnamon
1/4 teaspoon salt
1/2 cup raisins
1/2 teaspoon lemon peel
1 tablespoon lemon juice
1 unbaked 9-inch pie crust (see Cherry Settle's Pie Crust—page 167).

1. Preheat oven to 400° F.
2. Combine granulated sugar, flour, cinnamon and salt with the pear and apple slices, mixing well.
3. Add the raisins, lemon peel and lemon juice. Mix well.
4. Turn into the unbaked pie crust.
5. Sprinkle topping (see page 173) over pie.
6. Bake at 400° F. for 15 minutes.
7. Cover with foil and continue to bake for another 20 or 30 minutes, or until apples are tender.

Yields one 9-inch pie.

TOPPING FOR PEAR-APPLE CRUMB PIE

1/2 cup flour
1/2 cup brown sugar
1/2 teaspoon salt
1/2 cup chopped nuts (walnuts or pecans)
4 tablespoons butter

1. Combine flour, brown sugar and salt.
2. Cut in the butter until the mixture is crumbly.
3. Stir in the chopped nuts.
4. Use as directed.

Everyone looks forward to pumpkin pie around Thanksgiving.

PUMPKIN PIE

1 9-inch prebaked pie crust (see Cherry Settle's Pie Crust—page 167)
2 cups canned pumpkin
2 cups milk
1 cup granulated sugar
2 eggs, lightly beaten
2 teaspoons cinnamon
1 teaspoon allspice
1/2 teaspoon nutmeg
1/4 teaspoon cloves
1/4 teaspoon salt
2 tablespoons butter

1. Preheat oven to 450° F.
2. Combine pumpkin and sugar, blending thoroughly. Set aside.
3. Melt the butter in the milk over low heat.
4. Add milk to pumpkin mixture.
5. Add the eggs.
6. Season with the cinnamon, allspice, nutmeg, cloves and salt and put mixture in the pie crust.
7. Bake at 450° F. for 10 minutes.
8. Reduce heat to 350° F. and continue baking for 20 or 25 minutes, or until a knife inserted in the filling comes out clean.

Makes one 9-inch pie.

From the kitchen of Marge Stucker comes this version of an old favorite.

PUMPKIN PECAN PIE

1 cup canned pumpkin
3 eggs, slightly beaten
1 cup granulated sugar
1/2 cup dark corn syrup
1 teaspoon vanilla
1/2 teaspoon cinnamon
1/4 teaspoon salt
1 cup chopped pecans
1 unbaked 9-inch pie crust (see Cherry Settle's Pie Crust—page 167)

1. Preheat oven to 350° F.
2. Combine pumpkin, eggs, sugar and corn syrup.
3. Add the vanilla, cinnamon and salt and mix thoroughly.
4. Pour into the unbaked pie crust and top with pecans.
5. Bake at 350° F. for about 40 minutes or until knife inserted comes out clean.
6. Chill and serve topped with whipped cream.

Make one 9-inch pie.

BREADS

This was a Blue-ribbon winner at the Shelby County (Ky.) Fair (1976).

BANANA NUT BREAD

3 cups mashed bananas
1 cup granulated sugar
1/2 cup melted butter, or margarine
1 teaspoon baking soda
1/2 teaspoon salt
2 eggs, beaten
1-1/2 cups sifted flour
1 cup chopped pecans (or walnuts)

1. Preheat oven to 350° F.
2. Mix all ingredients in order.
3. Bake at 350° F. for one hour in greased and floured 8-1/2x4-1/2x2-5/8-inch loaf pan.

Yields 1 loaf.

Our customers like these with the soup course.

CORN MUFFINS

2 cups white corn meal
3/4 cup flour
1 teaspoon salt
1/2 cup sugar
2 eggs
1 teaspoon baking powder
3/4 cup shortening
3-1/4 cups buttermilk

Mix all ingredients together and bake about 10 minutes in greased muffin pan at 425° F.

Yields approximately 24 muffins.

Of such muffins do cooks dream.

BRAN MUFFINS

1 cup 100% bran buds
2 cups 40% bran flakes
1 cup boiling water
3/4 cup corn oil margarine
2-1/2 cups sifted flour
1 teaspoon salt
2-1/2 teaspoons baking soda
1-1/4 cups granulated sugar
2 eggs, beaten
2 cups buttermilk

1. Preheat oven to 400° F.
2. Pour boiling water over bran buds and let cool. Set aside.
3. In large mixing bowl combine margarine, sugar and eggs.
4. Beat for 2 minutes at medium speed.
5. Add buttermilk while beating at low speed for 1 minute.
6. Add bran flakes.
7. Sift in flour, salt, and baking soda.
8. Beat for 2 minutes.
9. Fold in bran buds by hand.
10. To use—drop by spoonfuls (don't stir batter) into greased muffin tins until 2/3 full.
11. Bake at 400° F. for 20 minutes.

Yields 2 quarts batter which may be used immediately or refrigerated.

Everyone likes biscuits and gravy. Or, try these with plenty of butter when they are fresh-baked and hot.

BUTTERMILK BISCUITS

2 cups sifted all-purpose flour
3/4 cup buttermilk
1-3/4 tablespoons baking powder
pinch of baking soda
1 teaspoon granulated sugar
1/2 teaspoon salt
3 tablespoons vegetable shortening

1. Preheat oven to 450° F.
2. Sift flour, baking powder, baking soda, salt and sugar together.
3. Cut in the shortening and mix thoroughly.
4. Add buttermilk gradually while continuing to mix.
5. Roll out on floured board and cut into biscuits.
6. Bake at 450° F. for 8 minutes.

Makes 8 to 12 biscuits depending on size.

Add variety to your meat dish with these dumplings which are easy to make.

ROBERTA K. KLEMM'S DUMPLINGS

1 egg, beaten
2/3 cup milk
1-3/4 cups sifted flour
1/2 teaspoon salt
1 teaspoon baking powder

1. Sift flour, salt and baking powder together. Set aside.
2. Combine egg and milk.
3. Add egg and milk mixture to flour mixture.
4. Stir until thoroughly blended.
5. Drop by tablespoons into boiling salted water, chicken broth or hot gravy and cook for 15 minutes.

Yields 10 dumplings.

This is a little trouble to prepare, but the raves you will receive will make it worth the effort.

MONKEY BREAD

1 envelope active dry yeast or 1 cake yeast
1/2 cup very warm water
1 cup butter (2 sticks)
1/2 cup granulated sugar
1 teaspoon salt
3-1/2 cups sifted, regular flour
1/2 cup evaporated milk

1. Sprinkle or crumble yeast into very warm water in a large bowl. Stir until dissolved.
2. Melt one-half cup butter in a small saucepan and stir in sugar, salt and evaporated milk until sugar dissolves.
3. Add yeast mixture.
4. Beat in flour all at once until batter is smooth and very stiff. Then knead until shiny-elastic.
5. Cover with a clean towel and let rise in a warm place away from draft for one hour, or until bulk is double.
6. Melt remaining butter in a small saucepan and set aside.
7. Punch dough down and roll into a rectangle 18x12-inches on a lightly floured pastry cloth or board; cut into diamond shapes with about 3-inch cutter.
8. Dip each piece of dough into the melted butter to coat both sides; place overlapping in layers in an ungreased 12-cup tube pan.
9. Cover and let rise again for 1 hour or until bulk is double.
10. Bake at 350° F. in preheated oven for 45 minutes or until golden brown. (Loaf should have a hollow sound when tapped).
11. Remove from pan.

Makes 1 loaf.
This is best served when warm.

This nut bread will make your cup of coffee taste better.

NUT BREAD

3 cups sifted all-purpose flour
1/2 cup brown sugar (firmly packed)
1/2 cup granulated sugar
2 tablespoons soft shortening
1 egg, beaten
1-1/2 cups evaporated milk
1/2 cup water
3-1/2 teaspoons baking powder
1 teaspoon salt
3/4 cup coarsely chopped pecans

1. Preheat oven to 350° F.
2. Blend flour, sugars, salt, baking powder, egg and shortening in a large mixing bowl.
3. Stir in water and milk until well blended.
4. Add nuts.
5. Pour into lightly greased and floured 10-1/2x5x3-inch loaf pan.
6. Let stand for 20 minutes.
7. Bake at 350° F. for one hour.
8. Remove from oven and let stand for about five minutes.
9. Turn out on a rack to cool.

Makes one loaf.

Surprise your family at breakfast with this extra-special treat.

NUT STREUSEL

Cake batter:
    1-1/2 cups sifted flour
    3 teaspoons baking powder
    3/4 cup granulated sugar
    1/4 cup butter
    1 egg, beaten
    1/2 cup milk
    1 teaspoon vanilla
    1/2 teaspoon salt

Nut topping:
    1/2 cup brown sugar
    2 tablespoons flour
    2 tablespoons melted butter
    1-1/2 teaspoons cinnamon
    3/4 cup pecans or walnuts, chopped

To prepare topping, blend all ingredients thoroughly.

1. Preheat oven to 350° F.
2. Sift flour, salt, baking powder and sugar together.
3. Work in butter; set aside.
4. In another dish, combine egg, milk and vanilla.
5. Add flour mixture.
6. Pour one-half of batter into well-greased 8x8-inch pan and sprinkle with half of the topping.
7. Add remaining batter.
8. Top this with remaining topping.
9. Bake at 350° F. for 25 to 35 minutes.

Yields one 8x8-inch cake.

Your children will really love the taste of this bread.

PEANUT BUTTER BREAD

1/2 cup peanut butter
1/2 cup brown sugar
1 teaspoon salt
1 cake yeast, or 1 package active dry yeast
1-1/2 cups scalded milk
1/4 cup warm water
4-1/2 cups sifted flour
1 egg, beaten

1.   In large bowl combine peanut butter, sugar, salt and scalded milk.
2.   Beat well for at least one minute and set aside to cool to lukewarm.
3.   Dissolve yeast in warm water.
4.   Add yeast mixture to peanut butter mixture.
5.   Add egg.
6.   Gradually add 4 cups of the flour, mixing thoroughly.
7.   Knead dough on floured board and add the remaining one-half cup flour.
8.   Place dough in greased bowl and let rise to double in size. Keep warm and out of draft.
9.   Knead again and shape into loaf in 9-1/2x5-1/2x2-3/4-inch greased pan.
10. Bake in preheated 375° F. oven for 35 to 45 minutes.
11. If you wish you may shape dough into 2 dozen rolls instead of one loaf. In this case bake for 20 to 25 minutes at 375° F.

Yields one loaf or 24 rolls.

The skim milk helps keep these pancakes thin.

ED KLEMM'S LIGHT PANCAKES

1/2 cup sifted flour
1-1/4 cups skim milk
1 egg, well beaten
2 teaspoons granulated sugar
1/4 teaspoon salt
1-1/2 teaspoons baking powder
1 tablespoon melted butter

1. Sift flour, salt, sugar and baking powder together. Set aside.
2. In separate dish, add milk and butter to egg.
3. Combine flour and egg mixtures.
4. Beat with rotary beater for one minute.
5. Fry on well-greased griddle that is not too hot. Turn pancakes once and remove when golden brown.

We suggest one tablespoon batter for each pancake. Stir batter often to keep from settling while using.
You might like to try a very thin slice of apple placed on top of each pancake as soon as it is poured.

Makes 35 small pancakes.

Roberta K. Klemm's recipe for popovers. To assure success, beat thoroughly and bake correctly.

POPOVERS

1 cup flour
1/4 teaspoon salt
1/4 teaspoon baking powder
1 cup milk
2 eggs
1 teaspoon melted butter, or margarine

1. Preheat oven to 450° F.
2. Sift flour, salt and baking powder together.
3. Slowly stir in the milk. Set aside.
4. Beat eggs well and add melted butter.
5. Add egg mixture to flour mixture and beat hard with a rotary mixer for three minutes.
6. Pour into preheated, greased custard cups, or into sizzling hot, heavy metal muffin pans, filling about 3/4 full.
7. Bake at 450° F. for 15 minutes, or until popovers are puffed.
8. Reduce heat to 350° F. and continue cooking for another 15 minutes, or until popovers are browned.

Yields seven large popovers.

These yeast rolls are easy to make and are delicious when served warm. They are a real favorite at the Dinner House.

YEAST ROLLS

4 cups sifted flour
3/4 cup lard or shortening
1 tablespoon salt
2 eggs
1 tablespoon sugar
1-1/3 cups water
1 cake yeast

1. Preheat oven to 425° F.
2. Dissolve yeast in 1/3 cup warm water.
3. Cream eggs, salt, sugar, shortening.
4. Add remainder of ingredients together with yeast mixture.
5. Roll into three small balls and place together in greased muffin pans. Let rise.
6. Bake in preheated 425° oven for 15 to 20 minutes.

Yields 24 rolls.

We think you will agree this is one of the best spoon breads you have ever tasted. The grits keep it moist and tasty.

SPOON BREAD

1/2 cup sifted flour
3/4 cup corn meal
1/2 teaspoon salt
1 teaspoon baking powder
1 teaspoon granulated sugar
1 cup milk
1/4 cup butter
1 egg
1 cup cooked grits

1. Preheat oven to 350° F.
2. Mix flour, corn meal, salt, baking powder and sugar; set aside.
3. Whip egg and milk together and whip into dry mixture.
4. Melt butter and blend in.
5. Add cooked grits. Don't let grits get too stiff. If they are thick, thin with a little cream.
6. Pour into a greased and hot pan, or casserole dish. Mixture should be at least 2-inches deep.
7. Bake at 350° F. for 35 minutes or until well set.

Serves 6 to 8.

You can taste the honey in this delicious, old-fashioned bread. If you like your crust soft, brush with melted butter or margarine before baking.

WHITE BREAD

2-3/4 cups all-purpose flour
1 cake yeast
1 teaspoon salt
1/2 cup lukewarm milk
1 egg, well beaten
1 tablespoon honey
2 tablespoons melted butter, or margarine

1. Sift flour and salt together. Set aside.
2. Dissolve yeast in milk and combine with egg and honey.
3. Add the melted butter and pour this mixture into the flour slowly.
4. Knead for at least five minutes.
5. Let rise to double its bulk.
6. Knead again slightly and place loaf in an 8-1/2x5-1/2x2-1/2-inch bread pan.
7. Let rise well above top of pan.
8. Bake in preheated 450° F. oven for 30 minutes.

Makes one loaf.

This is a must with your roast beef.

YORKSHIRE PUDDING

3 eggs
1 cup flour
1 cup milk
1/4 teaspoon salt
1/4 cup melted butter, or fat from cooking roast beef

1. Preheat oven to 450° F.
2. Sift flour and salt together.
3. Add milk gradually and stir to make a smooth mixture.
4. Add eggs.
5. Beat with a rotary egg beater for at least two minutes.
6. Pour melted butter, or grease from roast beef, into a baking pan. (Be sure sides are greased well.)
7. Pour pudding in pan to about 1/2-inch deep.
8. Bake at 450° F. for about 15 minutes.
9. Decrease heat to 375° F. and continue baking for 30 minutes.

Serves 6.

If you can't get your kids to eat vegetables, here's one way they will.

ZUCCHINI BREAD

3 eggs
2 cups granulated sugar
1 cup vegetable oil
2 cups grated, peeled *raw* zucchini
3 tablespoons vanilla extract
3 cups sifted all-purpose flour
1 teaspoon salt
1 teaspoon baking soda
1/4 teaspoon double-acting baking powder
2 teaspoons ground cinnamon
1 cup coarsely chopped pecans or walnuts
2 tablespoons grated orange rind

1. Preheat oven to 350° F.
2. Beat eggs until light and foamy.
3. Add sugar, oil, zucchini and vanilla and mix lightly, but well.
4. In a separate dish combine flour, salt, soda, baking powder and cinnamon and add to the egg-zucchini mixture.
5. Stir until well blended.
6. Add nuts and orange rind.
7. Pour into 2 greased 9x5x3-inch loaf pans.
8. Bake at 350° F. for one hour.
9. Cool on a rack.

Yields 2 loaves.

COLONEL SANDERS' SECRET RECIPE

So secret that neither the author nor the publisher knows what the recipe is.

MISCELLANEOUS

You might not need this often, but when you do you will find it a useful stock to be able to prepare.

COUNTRY HAM STOCK

2 Claudia Sanders Kentucky Country Ham hocks plus 1/2 pound ham skin
3 pints water
1/2 cup chopped celery
1 small chopped onion
1 medium-sized chopped carrot
1 teaspoon salt
1/2 teaspoon black pepper

1. Bring ham hocks and skin to a boil in three pints of water. Boil for 15 minutes.
2. Skim and add the celery, onion, carrot, salt and black pepper.
3. Boil for another 15 minutes.
4. Strain to remove solids and obtain stock.

Yields about 2-3/4 pints stock.

This is an easy stock to prepare and always seems to come in handy.

CHICKEN STOCK

1 small chicken cut up for boiling
3 pints water
1/2 cup chopped celery
1 small chopped onion
1 medium-sized chopped carrot
1 teaspoon salt
1/4 teaspoon white pepper

1. Bring chicken to a boil in three pints of water. Boil for twenty minutes.
2. Skim the liquid and add the celery, onion, carrot, salt and white pepper.
3. Boil for another 15 minutes.
4. Strain to remove solids and obtain the chicken stock.

Yields about 2-3/4 pints stock.

This is another useful stock.

MEAT STOCK

1 pound beef
3 pints water
1/2 cup chopped celery
1 small chopped onion
1 medium-sized chopped carrot
1 teaspoon salt
1/4 teaspoon black pepper

1. Bring meat to a boil in three pints of water. Boil for about 20 minutes.
2. Skim and add the celery, onion, carrot, salt and black pepper.
3. Boil for another 15 or 20 minutes.
4. Strain to remove solids and obtain meat stock.

Yields about 2-3/4 pints stock.

A good stuffing will add to the enjoyment of dining on roast chicken.

CHICKEN STUFFING I

18 biscuits (left over, or baked the day before)
1/4 cup chopped onion
1/2 cup chopped celery
1 teaspoon salt
1 teaspoon black pepper
1 teaspoon sage
1 cup water
1 teaspoon dry chicken soup base

1. Crumble biscuits into small pieces.
2. Add the onion, celery, salt, black pepper and sage. Mix thoroughly and set aside.
3. Mix the chicken soup base in the water and add this mixture to the biscuit mixture. Combine thoroughly.
4. Refrigerate overnight before using.

Makes enough dressing to stuff one chicken.

If you wish, you may add 1/2 teaspoon savory to this recipe.

CHICKEN STUFFING II

2 cups bread crumbs
1/4 cup finely chopped onion
1/2 cup finely chopped celery
1 tablespoon finely chopped parsley
1 egg, well beaten
3 tablespoons melted butter, or margarine
1/2 teaspoon salt
1/4 teaspoon black pepper
1/2 teaspoon thyme

1. In a saucepan, moisten the bread with two tablespoons of the butter, or margarine.
2. Add the egg, celery and parsley and mix thoroughly.
3. In a skillet, fry the onions in the remaining tablespoon of the butter, or margarine, until they begin to brown.
4. Season with the salt, black pepper and thyme and add to the bread mixture.

Makes enough dressing to stuff one chicken.

INDEX

CHAPTER 1

SOUPS AND APPETIZERS

CHAPTER II

SALADS

CHAPTER III

SALAD DRESSING AND SAUCES

CHAPTER IV

ENTRÉES

CHAPTER V

VEGETABLES

CHAPTER VI

DESSERTS, SAUCES, CONFECTIONS, CAKES AND PIES

CHAPTER VII

BREADS

CHAPTER VIII

MISCELLANEOUS